SERIAL KILLER TRIVIA

Fascinating Facts and Disturbing Details That Will Freak You the F*ck Out

MICHELLE KAMINSKY

Published in the US by:
ULYSSES PRESS
P.O. Box 3440
Berkeley, CA 94703
www.ulyssespress.com

ISBN: 978-1-61243-867-2
Library of Congress Control Number: 2018967987

Printed in Canada by Marquis Book Printing
10 9 8 7 6 5 4 3 2

Acquisitions editor: Casie Vogel
Managing editor: Claire Chun
Editor: Phyllis Elving
Proofreader: Barbara Schultz
Front cover design: Malea Clark-Nicholson
Artwork: from shutterstock.com: skull, lightning bolt, clouds, loose rope, bones
    © Ms Moloko; gun, handprint, handcuffs © Alena Gridushko; cleaver, poison,
    eyeball, hand, pill, ax © mhatzapa; rope, knife © Maria Gerasimova; branch,
    shovel, lighter, Christmas tree, square knot rope, flashlight, multitool, pickax,
    binoculars © Artspace; gas mask, pistol © ArnaPhoto

IMPORTANT NOTE TO READERS: Although the author and publisher have made every effort to ensure that the information in this book was correct at press time, the author and publisher do not assume and hereby disclaim any liability to any party for any loss, damage, or disruption caused by errors or omissions, whether such errors or omissions result from negligence, accident, or any other cause.

CONTENTS

INTRODUCTION

Since London newspapers made Jack the Ripper internationally famous in the late 19th century, serial killers have fascinated, terrified, and haunted us—and understandably so. These real-life monsters often lead ordinary lives, except for their penchant for seeking out and killing men, women, and/or children.

From Jeffrey Dahmer's cannibalism and preservation of victims' body parts to Aileen Wuornos' I-75 killing spree in Florida, many stories are stranger than any fiction even the most creative novelist could hope to write.

And so, whether in a quest to better understand these individuals and prevent similar crimes or simply out of morbid curiosity, we study their stories, from their (almost always) tragic and abusive childhoods to their heinous, murderous acts and, sometimes, to their own deaths, often at the hands of the government or fellow inmates.

Whatever your motivation is to learn more about serial killers, this book—organized into 150 questions and answers to enable you to take in as much or as little as you can stomach in one sitting—will supplement your knowledge. Within its pages, you will not only dive more deeply into the cases of some of the most notorious serial killers across the world but also read lesser-known stories nearly forgotten by history.

Now, lock your door, grab your favorite beverage, find a comfortable spot, and cuddle up with some of the most horrible humans the planet has ever seen.

Chapter 1

SERIAL KILLER BASICS

Q: Who invented the term "serial killer"?

A: People who have committed multiple murders have been around forever, and most of us probably can't remember a time when the term "serial killer" was not in use. But it didn't really enter the modern lexicon until the mid-1970s, when FBI criminal profiler Robert Ressler was a lecturer at a police academy in Bramshill, England.

In 1974 Ressler equated a rash of rapes, murders, arsons, and robberies with the serial adventure movies that were popular Sunday matinee fare in the 1930s and 1940s. Think legendary characters such as Dick Tracy, Tarzan, and Zorro, who carried out a new story line each week but always left viewers—often young boys—with unresolved plots to entice them back to the theater the following week.

Ressler reasoned that, just as in these film series, repeat killers heightened the tension with each "installment" of their murders, only increasing their desire to return to their basest desires again and again, perhaps even to perfect their crime. Their "serial" killing, then, wouldn't seem to have an end without either their own death or the intervention of law enforcement.

Before we used "serial killer" to describe multiple murders, the common term was "mass murderer," making the crimes sound far more random than the usually more calculated serial killings.

In 2014 Harold Schechter, author of several serial killer–themed books, came across what he believes to be the first use of the term "serial killer," dating to the 1930s in Germany. The director of the Berlin Criminal Police, Ernst August Ferdinand Gennat, used the term "*serienmörder*" in reference to the case of Peter Kürten, the Vampire of Düsseldorf. Margaret Seaton Wagner translated this as "serial murder" in her 1933 book *The Monster of Düsseldorf*.

The answer to the original question, though, cannot be complete without mention of Ressler's FBI colleague and fellow profiler John E. Douglas, who co-authored the book *Mindhunter: Inside the FBI's Elik Serial Crime Unit* with Mark Olshaker. Yes, the Netflix true crime drama *Mindhunter* and main character Holden Ford are based on Douglas, his book, and his experiences. In the show, the term "serial killer" first comes from the mouth of Bill Tench—the character based on Ressler—after he and Ford decide they need new terminology for a killer like Edmund Kemper.

Ressler and Douglas dedicated their professional lives to researching and writing about serial killers. They conducted countless one-on-one interviews with some of the most notorious serial killers of our time, including Ted Bundy, Jeffrey Dahmer, and Charles Manson, and delved into the psychology behind their murderous acts.

Ressler died in 2013, while Douglas continues to research and write about true crime. Most recently, he co-authored *The Killer Across the Table: Unlocking the Secrets of Serial Killers and Predators with the FBI's Original Mindhunter* (2019), again with Olshaker.

Q: Which country has had the most serial killers?

A: Raise up those American flags, because the answer is USA! USA! USA! The sad truth is that no other country even comes close.

The United States lays claim to 3,204 serial killers from 1900 to 2016, while the mother country of England comes in second at a mere 166. Yes, you math whizzes, that means the US tally is nearly 20 times that of the next closest country.

Are Americans just an exceptionally murderous people? Dr. Mike Aamodt, who runs the Serial Killer Information Center at Virginia's Radford University, doesn't think so.

Aamodt opines that two factors contribute to the skewed numbers: (1) law enforcement personnel in the US are skilled at both discovering homicides and linking them to the same killer; and (2) the country's expansive open records policies facilitate the crime-solving process by making information readily available to the public.

Aamodt also points to the overall murder rate in the US compared to other countries as further evidence that maybe the US isn't a hotbed of serial killing—the land of Uncle Sam falls somewhere in the middle of those stats.

Q: What is the most common murder method used by serial killers?

A: The answer may surprise you because it seems so impersonal, detached, and ordinary, but the method used most often by serial killers is the good ole gun. Shootings account for nearly half of the approximately 10,000 recorded serial murders in the US from 1900 up to the present.

The next most common method is strangulation, which has occurred in 22 percent of serial murders. Stabbing is third most frequent at around 15 percent.

Other reported methods, in order of frequency, include bludgeoning, poisoning, axing, drowning, smothering, burning, forced overdosing, and running over the victim with a vehicle.

Bombing doesn't make a statistical blip on the list, but the panic serial bombers can inspire makes it worth mentioning. Anyone would surely agree if they lived through the reigns of the Mad Bomber, George Metesky (New York City, 1940s and 1950s); the Unabomber, Ted Kaczynski (nationwide, 1978–1995); the Olympic Park Bomber, Eric Rudolph (Atlanta, Georgia, and Birmingham, Alabama, 1996–98); or Mark Anthony Conditt (Austin, Texas, 2018).

Q: Who is the typical serial killer in terms of sex, race, and intelligence?

A: You're probably not surprised to learn that men make up the vast majority of serial killers, nearly 90 percent. Whites account for the majority, but only just so at 52 percent; next come black serial killers at 40 percent. Other races are barely represented statistically: Hispanics at 7 percent, Native Americans at 1 percent, and Asians and less than 1 percent.

Regarding intelligence, although serial killers often have the reputation for being devious criminal masterminds, the reality is far more mundane—and so are their IQs. There are, of course, outliers. Edmund Kemper's 145 IQ qualifies him as "genius or near genius," and Ted Bundy's respectable 124 puts him at "very superior intelligence" on the IQ scale. For the most part, though, serial killers average an IQ of 94.5, which is perfectly "normal or average."

Something interesting does happen when IQ is considered in relation to the chosen method of killing. Those who chose bombing registered the highest average IQ among killing methods, at 140, while those who only bludgeoned victims (as opposed to bludgeoning along with another method) had the lowest average IQ, at 79.1.

Q: Are women equally represented among serial killers?

A: Ha! No.

While women comprise a little more than half the US population, they commit only 17 percent of serial killings in the US, which is obviously not close to equal. Interestingly, though, they commit just 10 percent of all murders in the country. That means that women actually commit a higher percentage of serial murders than other types of homicides. In other words, an American woman who has committed murder is actually more likely than not to be a serial killer.

And don't be fooled into thinking that women are always the reluctant or even unwilling accessories to their male partners. Sure, there are some—like the perpetrators of the Moors Murders, Ian Brady and Myra Hindley—who seem to fit that stereotype. But most female serial killers operate alone.

Sometimes the woman even drives the crimes. Craigslist Killer Miranda Barbour, for example, lured Troy LaFerrara to a mall parking lot in central Pennsylvania before killing him with the help of her husband of just three weeks, Elytte. Barbour said she had murdered 22 men over four states, though her claims haven't been verified.

For the most part, though, women serial killers work on their own, and they not only use different methods than male serial killers but also murder for different reasons. Women tend to kill people they know, while men usually choose victims at random from the general population.

Aileen Wuornos' spree of killing men she had just met is actually an outlier in the pattern of most women serial killers. In fact, disturbingly and ironically, many female serial killers are in trusted caretaker positions for their victims. Nurses such as Austria's Waltraud Wagner and her accomplices at the Lainz General Hospital fit this profile.

Looking at raw numbers, according to serial killer statistician extraordinaire Mike Aamodt, there have been 514 female serial killers since 1910. That's a lot, but it's not nearly the number of male serial killers recorded—4,200.

Is it possible that women serial killers just aren't caught as often as their male counterparts, making them vastly underestimated in crime statistics?

Maaaaybe?

Q: How many murders make someone a "serial killer"?

A: Although the term "serial killer" invokes images of a mad killing spree across months, years, or even decades, as far as the FBI is concerned a "serial killer" is anyone who murders more than one person in separate events.

That hasn't always been the only definition, though. Law enforcement officials, academics, researchers, and mental health professionals have categorized serial killers in several different ways over the past 40 years. For example, the old FBI definition included the requirement of a "cooling off period" between murders, and the Bureau once classified those without such a break as "spree killers." As of its 2005 Serial Murder Symposium, however, the FBI has settled on defining serial murder as "the unlawful killing of two or more victims by the same offender(s), in separate events."

The Symposium attendees—"a multidisciplinary group of experts"— aimed to create a simple but inclusive definition for law enforcement purposes, and the process outlined in the resulting report describes what must have been lively discussions among those in attendance. One can only imagine the intense debate over how many victims should be required to qualify as serial murder. On the one hand, academics and researchers preferred a specific number of victims for the ease of research, but law enforcement goals won out with the reasoning that a lower number of victims would give the police more latitude in committing department resources to catching perps.

But wait! If you answered "three or more" to the original question, you could also be considered correct. Current federal law that defines serial killings puts the requisite number of victims at three or more, at which point the FBI is legally permitted to assist local law enforcement agencies in pursuit of the killer.

So really, the correct answer may be more along the lines of "It depends on whom you ask."

Q: What are the four general categories of serial killer motives?

A: Ronald M. and Stephen T. Holmes are the authors of *Serial Murder*, in which they discuss two categories of serial killers: process-focused, who kill slowly, often through torture; and act-focused, who are concerned only with the murderous act itself.

The Holmes typology then breaks down these two categories into four—two process-focused and two act-focused—that separate serial killers according to their motivations.

PROCESS-FOCUSED SERIAL KILLERS

Hedonistic serial killers murder for the "fun" or thrill of it. Their victims are often random strangers, and death is usually swift and often nonsexual in nature. Carl "Coral" Watts was a classic hedonistic killer who reportedly took great pleasure in his acts, which included the murders of between 13 and 100 women.

Still in the hedonistic category, serial killers who gain sexual pleasure from torturing their victims—sometimes to the point of disfiguring them—are "lust killers." Russia's Elena Lobacheva, who killed 14 homeless people on Moscow streets, told authorities that "randomly stabbing the body of a dying human brought … pleasure compared to sexual pleasure." Lobacheva kept photos of her victims' mutilated bodies.

Also classified as hedonistic killers are "gain killers" who murder for financial profit. Organized crime hitmen and black widows—women who do away with their husbands or partners to inherit money or property—fall into this category.

Power-oriented serial killers are planners who tend to be psychopaths, though not psychotic. They ultimately seek control and domination, so rape is common among their crimes as it is an expression of power over the victim. So-called "angels of death," such as caretakers who kill patients in nursing homes, are considered power-oriented because they strive for control over the life and death of another.

Ted Bundy was largely motivated by power, though he also had lust killer tendencies. He fits squarely with one of the most common characteristics of power-oriented killers, that they tend to wear a "mask of sanity"—a term coined by psychiatrist Hervey Cleckley in 1941. They present an outward appearance of being mild-mannered, charming, charismatic, and generally upstanding citizens.

ACT-FOCUSED SERIAL KILLERS

Mission-oriented serial killers target specific groups—commonly prostitutes, Jews, blacks, the homeless, or homosexuals. These killers believe that certain groups are undesirable and undeserving of life. Lobacheva, mentioned above as a hedonistic lust killer, overlaps into this category as well.

Between 1977 and 1980, white supremacist and former Ku Klux Klan member Joseph Paul Franklin aimed his sniper's rifle at blacks across the country, killing more than 15 people and wounding several others. Franklin's mission was to eliminate "race mixing," which he believed to be "a sin against God and nature."

Visionary serial killers are usually psychotic, killing because of visions and/or voices that have instructed them to do so. At the trial of

Herbert Mullin, diagnosed with paranoid schizophrenia, his defense attorney told jurors in his opening statement that Mullin was "stark raving mad" and that he heard voices directing him to kill people as "human sacrifices" to prevent earthquakes.

Q: Are most serial killers legally insane?

A: Nope. Although many serial killers may be mentally ill, most do not meet the legal definition of insanity. In fact, that defense is rarely even invoked in serial killer proceedings.

When using the insanity defense, a defendant admits to the crimes charged but also claims he or she is not culpable because of mental illness. To escape criminal liability through legal insanity, in many jurisdictions defendants must show they couldn't have known what they were doing or that it was wrong. This standard is extremely difficult to meet even when the defendant has a clinically diagnosed mental illness, which is why it's rarely successful. Jeffrey Dahmer and John Wayne Gacy both tried to use the insanity defense but were ultimately convicted.

One notable exception to the general rule of the insanity plea's inefficacy is Ed Gein. Initially found to be incompetent to stand trial, Gein was tried ten years later and found guilty but legally insane in the 1957 murder of Bernice Worden. He spent the rest of his life at Central State Hospital in Waupun, Wisconsin.

Competency to stand trial, incidentally, is a separate legal concept that addresses whether someone has the mental capacity to understand the proceedings against them and aid in their own defense. Many defendants are deemed competent to stand trial even if they have been diagnosed with one or more mental illnesses.

For example, a psychiatric report said that David Berkowitz, the Son of Sam killer, was paranoid and delusional, but he was determined to be competent to stand trial. Berkowitz, of course, didn't ever stand trial, as he pleaded guilty against the recommendation of his attorney, who wanted him to plead insanity. Statistically speaking, though, he probably wouldn't have won by using that defense anyway.

Q: What three characteristics comprise the Macdonald triad?

A: The Macdonald triad consists of three characteristics that forensic psychiatrist J. M. Macdonald identified as most predictive of future violent behavior: fire-starting, enuresis (bed-wetting), and animal cruelty.

Macdonald's conclusion dates back to a 1963 paper called "The Threat to Kill," published in the *American Journal of Psychiatry*. His findings are based on the comparison of 48 psychotic patients and 52 non-psychotic patients at the Colorado Psychopathic Hospital in Denver, all of whom had threatened to kill but had not actually done so.

Three years after the paper's publication, Daniel S. Hellman and Nathan Blackman put Macdonald's theory to the test with 84 prisoners. Their findings seemed to confirm Macdonald's conclusions.

In the nearly 60 years since Macdonald's pronouncement, the triad has become heavily integrated in both criminology and psychology coursework. Heck, it's even been referenced in an episode of *Law and Order: Special Victims Unit*.

But that doesn't make it true.

Macdonald himself doubted his own theory in his 1968 book *Homicidal Threats*, and subsequent, more scientifically rigorous studies have failed to find a correlation between the triad and homicidal tendencies. Neurologist Jonathan H. Pincus, in his 2001 book *Base Instincts: What Makes Killers Kill?*, noted that the traits are really only indicative of childhood abuse and not a predictor of future violent behavior.

Sure, there are a lot of serial killers who have exhibited these traits—from Edmund Kemper's animal cruelty to Andrei Chikatilo's bed-wetting—but lots of kids who exhibit these behaviors also end up not being serial killers.

For anyone interested in reading more on this topic, an excellent overview is offered by Kori Ryan's 2009 thesis, "The Macdonald Triad: Predictor of Violence or Urban Myth?" Spoiler alert: Ryan finds "little empirical support" for the theory's validity.

Still, bonus points if you knew that the Macdonald triad may also be called the "homicidal triad," the "Hellman and Blackman triad," or the "triad of sociopathy."

Q: Where is Murderville, USA?

A: In February 1973, after the bloodied bodies of four young men were discovered in a makeshift cabin in California's Henry Cowell Redwoods State Park, the district attorney of Santa Cruz County was quoted in newspapers as saying, "We must be the murder capital of the world right now."

One story floating around the Internet says that DA Peter Chang actually said "Murderville, USA," but the reporter jotted down and then wrote "murder capital of the world," which got picked up around the country. But that wouldn't explain how the term "Murderville, USA" made it into serial killer lore.

The February 18, 1973 edition of the *San Francisco Examiner* offers a clue. Staff writer Don West's story about the discovery of the young men's bodies starts on the front page, but its second part is buried on page 28 and found under the headline "Santa Cruz' Title—Murderville?" Perhaps, then, West is to be credited for this turn of phrase.

Chang's statement—regardless of which version is true—was hyperbole, of course, but those four murders in just the second month of 1973 brought the total homicides in Santa Cruz County up to 13 for the year. The city of Santa Cruz in the 1970s had a population of just 30,000 to 40,000, but it was certainly a hotbed of serial killing, with John Linley Frazier (the Killer Prophet), Edmund Kemper (the Co-Ed Killer), and Herbert Mullin all targeting victims in and around the city.

By February 1973, Frazier had already been convicted of the 1970 murders of Dr. Victor Ohta and his wife, Virginia; their two sons (Derrick,

12, and Taggart, 11) and Ohta's secretary, Dorothy Cadwallader. The murders had occurred just two miles from the site of the cabin where the four young men were found.

Mullin had been arrested two days prior to the gruesome discovery in the mountains around Santa Cruz, charged with six previous murders in 1973, while Kemper's indictment on eight counts of murder would come in May of that same year.

Sidenote: In addition to either coining or inspiring the term "Murderville, USA," Chang holds a special place in serial killer trivia for another reason. The Stanford law graduate, who at 28 was the youngest district attorney in the country when elected and the only Asian American to hold that position, personally prosecuted both Frazier and Kemper. He was slated to prosecute Mullin as well but fell ill with appendicitis and was unable to do so.

Q: Who is the Houston-based victims' rights advocate who has waged war on "murderabilia"?

A: Andy Kahan is a New York native and former parole officer who has been battling against what he calls "murderabilia" for the better part of three decades. Buying and selling objects connected with grisly crimes has become a huge business, with collectors scrambling for such macabre items as handwritten and hand-signed letters by Green River Killer Gary Ridgway, Charles Manson's prison-owned dentures, and locks of Aileen Wuornos' hair.

Kahan believes the selling of serial killer mementos causes unnecessary pain for victims' loved ones and sensationalizes violent crime. He'd like to see federal legislation enacted to stop it, and that's not an impossible goal—Kahan was instrumental in pushing through the Texas "Son of Sam" law prohibiting criminals from profiting from their crimes within the state's borders.

"Son of Sam," of course, refers to serial killer David Berkowitz, who inspired the original version of this type of law in New York in the late 1970s. Besides New York and Texas, six other states have similar legislation, and Kahan has spent considerable time traveling around the country toting a duffel bag full of his own murderabilia collection, encouraging the remaining jurisdictions to pass laws as well.

After the self-labeled "Man in Black" was appointed to the newly created position of Victim Advocate for the City of Houston in 1992, he molded his role into one that incorporated traditional advocacy and lobbying, with a media blitz that brought attention to many "glitches and wrongdoings in the criminal justice system." Among the latter is the disturbing practice of criminals benefiting financially from their crimes.

During Kahan's tenure, he fought for the passing of more than 20 pieces of legislation that covered all kinds of victim rights. These included giving murder victims' loved ones the opportunity to watch executions and allowing domestic violence and sexual assault victims to apply for relocation expenses from the Crime Victim Compensation Fund.

Kahan announced his retirement from government office in the summer of 2018, but he quickly hopped over to the private Crime Stoppers of Houston, where he assumed the role of the Director of Victim Services and Advocacy.

No matter where Kahan's office is technically located, there's little doubt that this impassioned, sardonic, and downright feisty victims' advocate will continue making a difference. Whether he keeps building his duffel bag collection of murderabilia remains to be seen.

Q: Some believe serial killers are "bad seeds," born evil. Where does this term come from?

A: William March coined the term in the title of his 1954 psychological horror novel *The Bad Seed*, which was the basis of the 1956 Academy Award–nominated film of the same name. The novel was also adapted into a wildly successful Broadway play. Perhaps not many people these days have heard of it, but the book was critically acclaimed in its time and was nominated for the National Book Award for Fiction in 1955. A *New York Herald Tribune* critic called it "[d]ark, original, [and] ultimately appalling."

The Bad Seed is about an eight-year-old girl named Rhoda Penmark whose mother, Christine, begins to wonder whether the tragic drowning death of Rhoda's classmate Claude was really an accident. Christine investigates on her own upon seeing Rhoda's indifference to Claude's demise and catches Rhoda in a lie about when she had last seen the boy. She also discovers that Rhoda had been arguing with Claude just before he drowned, and that his face had unexplained crescent-shaped marks on it.

At this point Christine starts to recall curious incidents involving Rhoda, including the "accidental" deaths of a puppy and an elderly neighbor who had promised the little girl a prized piece of jewelry. Now suspicious, Christine questions her adoptive father about her own birth mother—who, it turns out, was a serial killer executed for her crimes. Christine fears she has passed along the genetic predisposition to kill and has delivered a bad seed into the world. She writes a series of letters to her husband about what she has learned, but never sends them.

Thereafter, Christine witnesses her daughter lock the apartment maintenance man, Leroy Jessup, in a room and set it on fire. It turns out that Jessup had also discovered Rhoda's dark side when he cracked the mystery of Claude's death by joking with the young girl that she must have beaten the boy to death with her shoe, leaving those marks on his face.

Christine confronts her daughter, who eventually confesses to the murders of Claude, Jessup, and the neighbor, and the mother takes the extreme measure of giving Rhoda an overdose of sleeping pills so she could never kill again. Then Christine shoots herself in the head—but not before destroying the letters she had written about Rhoda's crimes.

The landlady hears the gunshot, however, and arrives in time to save Rhoda. With Christine now gone, only Rhoda knows what she has done—and she is in the clear to strike again.

Q: What do you call a male "black widow"?

A: Everyone knows the term "black widow" to describe women who kill their own partners — usually husbands, but sometimes lovers. But what if a man targets his partner in this way? A man who has murdered more than one of his partners is a "Bluebeard," a term derived from the blue-black facial hair of Gilles de Rais. A French knight and lord who fought alongside Joan of Arc, de Rais killed hundreds of young boys in 15th-century France.

But wait, you're thinking, de Rais didn't kill any of his wives or lovers! In fact, he was never even accused of such atrocities. The hue of his beard is forever connected with serial killers, though, because he is believed to have been the inspiration for Charles Perrault's fairy tale "Bluebeard."

In "Bluebeard," the beautiful wives of a powerful yet hideous nobleman keep disappearing. Married once again, he leaves the country, but not before giving his new young wife the keys to his house with the strict instructions that she is not to enter a closed-off underground chamber. Probably before Bluebeard's carriage was even out of the driveway, the wife ventures into the forbidden room and finds it full of blood, with the bodies of Bluebeard's former wives hanging on the walls. She drops the key in horror and then can't get it clean, à la Lady MacBeth.

She tells her sister, who is staying with her, and they plan to leave the next day. But Bluebeard returns unexpectedly, finds the bloody key, and knows he has been found out. The wife stalls by asking for a final prayer with her sister, and just as Blackbeard is ready to kill both of them, their brothers barge in and kill Bluebeard.

The wife inherits Bluebeard's fortune and property, uses her money to marry off her siblings, and remarries a man she loves. In sum, they all (well, except for Bluebeard and all the dead wives) live happily ever after.

Heckuva fairy tale, eh?

The term "Bluebeard" has largely fallen out of favor in recent years—but if you happen to be a perspicacious Netflix viewer, you may have noticed that the 2018 season finale of *You*, the psychological thriller featuring a serial killer, was called "Bluebeard's Castle."

You can probably guess how that episode ends.

Q: Whose basement holds the brain of John Wayne Gacy?

A: Dr. Helen Morrison has kept Gacy's brain in formaldehyde in a secured area of her basement since 1994. A forensic psychiatrist, she is the author of *My Life Among Serial Killers: Inside the Minds of the World's Most Notorious Murderers*—and when she says "inside the minds," she means that literally.

Before Gacy's execution in 1994, Morrison had interviewed him extensively, spending approximately 50 hours with him while forming the expert opinion that he was legally insane. At the murder trial, Morrison testified for the defense that Gacy would have committed those heinous acts even "if the president of the United States was there with him at the time."

Before his death, Gacy expressed the wish that scientists study his brain, and Morrison got a release from his family to cart it away after his autopsy; she also has pieces of all his organs. Researchers have studied Gacy's brain over the years but haven't found anything out of the ordinary—certainly nothing that would indicate the depravity that went on up there while Gacy was alive.

Morrison has dedicated her professional career to better understanding the psyches and brain functions of serial killers, especially searching for common characteristics. One of her conclusions is that serial killers generally tend to be stunted in their emotional development at the infant stage. She cites damage to the hypothalamus as a potential link with both a lack of emotional maturity and a propensity toward violence.

In addition to Gacy, she has profiled more than 135 other murderers around the world, including Ed Gein, Wayne Williams, and Fred and Rosemary West.

Q: What genetic syndrome has been studied as a possible link with serial killing?

A: XYY syndrome or Jacobs syndrome, in which males have an extra Y chromosome, occurs approximately once in every 1,000 live births in the United States. During the 1960s the media ran erroneous reports that serial killer Richard Speck, who had brutally raped and murdered eight nursing students in 1966, had an extra Y chromosome. Chatter ensued that XYY syndrome makes afflicted males more prone to violence.

Well, scientific data never backed up that theory, and even by 1969, both the American Psychiatric Association and the National Institute of Mental Health were scrambling to set the scientific record straight. All subsequent research has led to the same conclusion: the behavior of males born with an extra Y chromosome probably is not significantly different from that of males born with only XY.

Sure, they may be taller than their XY counterparts, have more acne, and be more likely to have learning disabilities, but there has never been a link to increased criminal behavior. Still, several biology and psychology textbooks have incorporated the misleading information, and the stigma continues in pop culture. A 1993 *Law & Order* episode called "Born Bad" is about a 14-year-old sociopathic killer with an extra Y chromosome; his lawyer argues that he is not responsible for his crimes because of his extra Y chromosome.

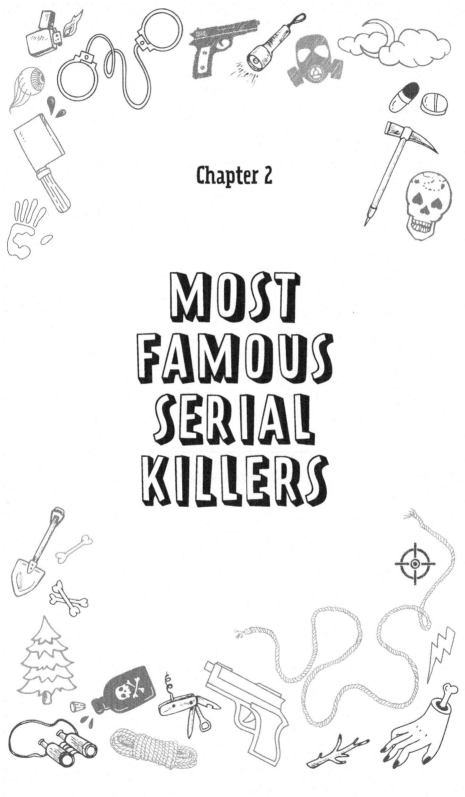

Chapter 2

MOST FAMOUS SERIAL KILLERS

Q: What foiled Jeffrey Dahmer's plan for creating the perfect zombie sex slave?

A: Despite the fact that his father was a chemist and Dahmer himself had been experimenting with hydrochloric acid for years, he apparently did not guess that the acid he dripped into holes drilled in his still-living victims' brains would kill them within two days.

Go figure.

After murdering and dismembering several men he had brought home for sex, Dahmer turned to performing crude lobotomies; killing and disposing of bodies and constantly seeking new victims had become rather impractical. During his sanity trial, Dr. Frederick Fosdal testified that the serial killer lamented having to step over bodies in the tub while he showered.

Dahmer wanted to be able to control his victims sexually, so he came up with the sex zombie idea—which, Fosdal rather bizarrely noted, "could have been successful" and "would have been a solution to his dilemma."

Dahmer's path to serial killing was paved with such common denominators as sexual molestation when he was a young boy and the contentious separation and divorce of his parents. By age 10, young Dahmer was already collecting roadkill, dismembering dead animals, and experimenting with acid to bleach chicken bones.

Just after Dahmer's high school graduation, the future serial killer brought 19-year-old Steven Hicks home to the family residence, where he was living alone at the time. He had sex with Hicks and then bludgeoned him with a barbell, strangled him, and dismembered and buried his body. Afraid the corpse would be found, as Dahmer admitted years later, he dug it up, dissolved the skin and organs in acid, crushed the bones, and sprinkled what was left outdoors.

Dahmer didn't kill again for several years, instead piling up charges of indecent exposure and disorderly conduct for masturbating in public. After a short stint in the army he was booted out for boozing too much; he'd had to leave Ohio State University for similar reasons. In 1987 Dahmer killed again, though until he confessed years later the authorities didn't link him to the murder of Steven Tuomi, whose heart he had tried to pull from his chest with his bare hands.

In 1989—after having killed at least three more victims—Dahmer was convicted of the sexual assault of a young boy; he served 10 months of a one-year sentence. Over the next decade he racked up nearly a dozen more victims but wasn't even suspected of any crimes until The Stench.

By July 1991, neighbors had been aware of horrible smells emanating from Dahmer's unit in the Oxford Apartments Complex in Milwaukee, Wisconsin, for more than a year. The quiet, lanky, blond dude who lived there always had an explanation—his freezer had conked out and all the meat had spoiled, there were dead mice stuck in the walls, he had sewage issues. Whatevs.

But the truth couldn't have been more horrific for the police who showed up after 32-year-old Tracy Edwards ran into the street, a handcuff still dangling from his wrist, and told police officers what he had seen and experienced in the gruesome Apartment 213.

Dahmer almost talked his way past the officers' suspicions, but they spotted some Polaroids of dismembered bodies, arrested him, and commenced with their search. Inside the apartment, police found albums full of images of body parts; heads in the refrigerator and freezer; a small collection of skulls; body parts decomposing in acid; and signs that Dahmer had been consuming some of his victims' organs. During his confession, Dahmer told police he had placed the heart of second-to-last victim, Oliver Lacy, in his refrigerator to "eat later."

In all, they recovered the remains of 11 male victims—nine black, one Laotian, and one white. Authorities determined that Dahmer's practice was to lure men to his apartment; have sex with and/or rape them, alive and/or dead; drug, strangle, and dismember them; and sometimes eat their body parts.

In the end, Dahmer's experiments in creating the perfect zombie sex slave were abject failures, and bloody, putrid Apartment 213 has to go down as one of the most disturbing crime scenes in history. With a total of 17 victims, all of whom surely had loved ones, it is unfathomable to think about how many lives Dahmer's rape, necrophilia, cannibalism, murder, and dismemberment ultimately affected.

Q: How did Jeffrey Dahmer almost get caught two months before he actually did?

A: In May 1991, neighbors saw a bloody, naked 14-year-old Laotian boy run from Dahmer's apartment building. Police arrived at the scene to find a dazed and disoriented Konerak Sinthasomphone, and they returned him to Dahmer's apartment. Dahmer fed them the story that Konerak was his drunk adult lover, and they had been fighting. And so the officers left the boy there.

Dahmer later admitted that when Konerak escaped from the apartment, he had already drilled a hole in his head and dripped acid into it. That certainly would explain Konerak's inability to communicate effectively with the police officers. Dahmer confessed that he strangled Konerak to death not long after police brought him back.

Konerak was the youngest child of a family that was seeking freedom from communist repression when they settled into a thriving Laotian community of 7,000 in Milwaukee in 1980. To escape from Laos, Konerak's father, Sounthone, had built a canoe and sent his family across the Mekong River to a refugee camp in Thailand, the youngest members drugged with sleeping pills so they wouldn't cry and alert soldiers to their presence. A few days later Sounthone swam to rejoin them. The family lived in the camp for a year before relocating to Milwaukee with the help of the local Catholic archdiocese.

Tragically, Konerak wasn't even the first member of his family to be a victim of Dahmer. One of Konerak's older brothers, who was 16 at the time of Konerak's death, was the boy Dahmer had sexually molested in 1988. Dahmer was convicted of that crime in 1989, but he wrote a letter of apology that appeared to be sincere and remorseful enough to convince Judge William Gardner to cut his one-year sentence short. Dahmer ended up spending only 10 months in prison and was released to kill again … and again … and again.

At his 1992 trial on 15 counts of murder, Dahmer pleaded insanity. Jurors weren't having it and found him both sane and guilty. He was sentenced to 15 consecutive life sentences, bringing the total number of years to nearly 1,000. He later pleaded guilty to the murder of Steven Hicks and had another life sentence tacked on.

Dahmer only made it about two and a half years in prison, though, before the first attempt on his life—a throat slashing by a fellow inmate in the prison chapel. Dahmer survived but still refused special protection. He met his demise several months later, in November 1994, when inmate Christopher Scarver bludgeoned him with a metal bar in a bathroom next to the prison gym.

Scarver said Dahmer would mold prison food into the shape of severed limbs, drizzle on ketchup to look like blood, and then place it where others would see it. The dude was creepy. In 2015 Scarver insisted that prison guards had facilitated his being alone with Dahmer so he could take care of him and his unnerving behavior.

Side note: The two officers who returned young Konerak to Dahmer, John A. Balcerzak and Joseph T. Gabrish, were fired from the police force but later reinstated after a judge awarded them $55,000 each in back pay. He called the termination decision "shocking to one's sense of fairness."

Q: What was John Wayne Gacy's last meal?

A: Gacy went out with a pound of strawberries and a pile of grease in the form of a bucket of Original Recipe Kentucky Fried Chicken, a dozen fried shrimp, and French fries. His execution by lethal injection took 18 minutes because one of the IV lines clogged and officials had to fix it. Reportedly his last words were "Kiss my ass."

Gacy had a special place in his heart for KFC, as he had managed his former father-in-law's three franchises in Waterloo, Iowa after graduating from college. During this time, Gacy was by all outward appearances a respectable citizen, the father of two children and especially active in the Jaycees.

His secret life was revealed in May 1968 when he was arrested and charged with coercing a 15-year-old male employee into homosexual acts over the course of several months. He then hired another teenager to beat up the young boy. Gacy ended up pleading guilty to sodomy and receiving a 10-year prison sentence. Because of his good behavior, though, he was released just 18 months later. In the meantime, his wife divorced him.

Gacy started his own construction business, but by 1971 he was facing new charges related to sexual acts with another young boy. Those were dropped when the teenager didn't show up for court. Gacy remarried in 1972—though sexual relations with his wife stopped early in the marriage—and began the side gig that would come to define his persona in the annals of serial killer history. As Pogo the Clown he appeared in full-on clown garb and makeup at children's parties and fundraisers.

Gacy's MO was always the same. He lured young men and boys to his house and showed them some magic tricks involving handcuffs. Then he used chloroform to sedate them before sodomizing them. Next came his "rope trick"—which ended with their strangulation. Gacy buried the bodies in a four-foot-deep, dirt-floored crawl space. The odor emanating from that area was what eventually led to his arrest.

In all, Gacy killed at least 33 young men and boys. His first known victim was 18-year-old Timothy McCoy in 1972, and his last was 15-year-old Robert Piest in 1978. Piest's disappearance from a pharmacy led police to Gacy when they discovered he had been in the store and had previously molested at least one young boy.

Q: What gift did John Wayne Gacy give to FBI profiler Robert Ressler?

A: After his capture and imprisonment, Gacy delved into art to pass the time—in fact, many of his works have become hot commodities on the murderabilia market and include oil and acrylic paintings as well as drawings of subjects ranging from Jesus Christ to the Seven Dwarfs. Gacy sent many pieces of his artwork to pen pals, but one painting found a special home with his favorite (probably) FBI profiler, Robert Ressler.

In one of Ressler's interviews with Gacy, the serial killer most associated with clowns because of his "Pogo" persona gifted Ressler with a brightly colored painting of himself as a clown. The inscription on the back read, "Dear Bob Ressler, you cannot hope to enjoy the harvest without first laboring in the fields. Best wishes and good luck. Sincerely, John Wayne Gacy, June 1988."

When Ressler asked Gacy what he meant by those cryptic words, Gacy replied, "Well, Mr. Ressler, you're the criminal profiler. You're the FBI. You figure it out."

Bonus trivia: At one fundraising event at which Gacy appeared as Pogo the Clown, he was photographed with future First Lady Rosalyn Carter, wife of the 39th president of the United States, Jimmy Carter.

Q: What testimony from Dr. Richard Souviron helped convict killer Ted Bundy?

A: In 1979, at the time of Bundy's trial for the death of two Florida State University sorority sisters, forensic science wasn't nearly as advanced as it is today. But Souviron, a dentist and forensic odontologist, testified that photographs and impressions of Bundy's teeth were a "perfect match" with the marks on 20-year-old Lisa Levy's buttocks.

In 1978, Bundy had busted into the Chi Omega house at FSU and, in a harried 15-minute span, brutally attacked four sleeping women and killed two of them, Levy and 21-year-old Margaret Elizabeth Bowman. The other two women survived, as did a fifth victim Bundy attacked in her off-campus apartment after she fled the sorority house.

In all, Bundy murdered at least 30 women between 1961 and 1978, making him one of the world's most prolific serial killers ever. He was also one of the sickest. He had a habit of returning to his victims' corpses to perform various sexual acts on them until the remains became too decomposed to do so.

If there were serial killer superlatives, Bundy would probably win as the most handsome, charming, and charismatic among the lot. He was also well educated; he had even gone to law school at the University of Utah, which came in handy when he represented himself during subsequent legal proceedings.

Bundy's socially positive attributes probably are what kept his horrifying crimes hidden for so long, but he couldn't run from the law forever. He was executed in Florida's electric chair in 1989 after a prison-standard last meal of steak and eggs with hash browns, toast with butter and jelly, milk, and juice.

Bundy's body was cremated and his ashes scattered over the Cascade Mountains in the state of Washington.

Q: Where can you see Ted Bundy's Volkswagen Beetle?

A: Bundy's 1968 Volkswagen Beetle, instrumental in bringing him to justice, is currently on display at the Alcatraz East Crime Museum in Pigeon Forge, Tennessee.

Bundy had put up the facade of an upstanding citizen for many years, but his secret life began to unravel when he didn't pull over for a cop in Utah in August 1975. Sergeant Bob Hayward, a 22-year veteran of the Utah Highway Patrol, noticed a strange car on his residential street at 2:30 a.m., so he put on his high beams so he could read the plate. The beige VW's lights flicked off and the car sped away. Hayward followed until its driver pulled into a vacant gas station parking lot.

When Hayward asked Bundy what he was doing out at that hour, Bundy's claim that he'd been to see the movie *Towering Inferno* didn't hold water, as Hayward knew the film wasn't playing anywhere nearby. He asked if he could have a look inside the car. After Bundy consented, Hayward noticed a missing passenger seat and a crowbar behind the driver's seat as well as what one might legitimately call a murder kit: wire, rope, a knit ski mask, another mask fashioned from pantyhose with cut-out eyes, handcuffs, and an ice pick.

By this point, Bundy had been kidnapping, assaulting, and murdering young women throughout Washington, Utah, Idaho, and Colorado for at least a year and a half—and his name had been floated around some police departments as a suspect. He was arrested for evading the police that August night, but they were unable to tie him to any crime and released him.

A week later authorities added the charge of possession of burglary tools. They even found gas station receipts linking him to the locations of missing women in Colorado, but there was still nothing concrete on which to hold him.

After cleaning the VW, Bundy sold it—surely thinking he was in the clear regarding the car. Alas for him, authorities later seized it from the new owner and performed forensic testing, which revealed hairs from three victims. One of them was Carol DaRonch, who had survived an attack and now identified Bundy as the perp who had pretended to be a police officer in Salt Lake City.

Bundy was convicted of the aggravated kidnapping of DaRonch in 1976 and sentenced to one to 15 years' confinement in the Utah State Prison. While incarcerated, he was charged with the murder of Caryn Campbell in Colorado, again thanks to forensic evidence recovered from the VW: hairs behind the back seat and blood under the door panel.

While awaiting trial in Colorado, Bundy escaped from custody twice. The first time, he jumped from the second story window of the courthouse's law library and was apprehended about a week later. After his second escape, he made it all the way to Tallahassee, where he murdered Florida State University college students Lisa Levy and Margaret Elizabeth Brown—the crimes for which he was ultimately executed.

Q: What evidence broke the case of the BTK killer, Dennis Rader?

A: The Bind, Torture, Kill murderer—alternately called the BTK Strangler—flew under the radar in Kansas for 30 years because Rader was seen as a loving father, Cub Scout leader, and church deacon.

But when he sent a floppy disk to police, he neglected to wipe identifying data such as the fact that "Dennis" had saved the last file and that someone had used the disk at Christ Lutheran Church. Rader had used the church computer to print the file because his own printer was broken. Whoopsie!

This was enough to lead Lieutenant Ken Landwehr and his fellow Wichita Police Department homicide detectives to Rader, who was president of the congregation. Before letting Rader know they were on to him, prosecutors convinced a court to subpoena a tissue sample taken from a Pap smear collected five years previously from Rader's daughter, when she was in college. They compared it with crime scene DNA that Landwehr had been instrumental in preserving, and the familial connection was clear. The community was stunned by Rader's arrest in February of 2005—31 years after he had committed the brutal murders of the Otero family in their Wichita home. The victims included 38-year-old Joseph Otero, his 33-year-old wife Julie, 11-year-old daughter Josephine, and 9-year-old son Joseph. The bodies were found by 15-year-old son Charlie.

The BTK Killer has been identified as the culprit in six additional murders, the last one in 1991. Authorities believe he may be responsible for more killings, as the 31-year gap is rare for serial killers. Rader was actually plotting a new murder at the time of his arrest. According to the FBI, between his last victim and his capture in 2005, the BTK Killer satisfied his urges with "autoerotic activities."

But nothing could satisfy the BTK Killer's ego and narcissism, and that's what Landwehr zeroed in on. When a *Wichita Eagle* article guessed that the killer was either dead or imprisoned, Rader couldn't stay quiet. He began sending letters and even puzzles to the media—10 of them in the year before his arrest.

Landwehr played on Rader's attention-seeking behavior and held multiple news conferences, poking at the unidentified killer to be in contact with police. Rader took the bait, and in one message he oddly solicited advice from the police about whether communicating by means of a floppy disk would be safe. Following Rader's instructions, the police took out a newspaper ad that said, "Rex, it will be OK." The killer sent the fated floppy a few weeks later, and the dominoes began to fall.

One of the most fascinating aspects of Rader's capture is how much he trusted the police and how comfortable he felt around them, even throughout the 32-hour interrogation during which he confessed in dreadful detail. At one point, the killer even requested that an officer mark "BTK" on his cup before placing it in the fridge. Rader was downright incredulous that Landwehr had steered him wrong. "How come you lied to me?" he repeatedly asked.

"The floppy did me in," Rader himself acknowledged. Now he has 10 life sentences in prison to think about what he's done.

Q: What Irish-American doctor was suspected of the Whitechapel Murders?

A: Known better as the crimes of Jack the Ripper, the Whitechapel Murders in London have put many, many men under suspicion for a case that is still unsolved more than 130 years later. One of the least known among the bunch was an Irish-American man, Dr. Francis Tumblety. According to the authors of *Jack the Ripper: America's First Serial Killer*, Tumblety was actually arrested for the crimes but slipped the continent when he was granted bail.

Stewart Evans and Paul Gainey write that Tumblety (alternately spelled Tumuelty, Tumility, and Twomblety) was a woman-hating snake oil salesman arrested by the British police in 1888 for the murders but then was let out on bail for lack of evidence. No one had heard of the "misogynistic quack," as John Pitcher of the Rochester *Democrat and Chronicle* called him, until 1993, when Evans discovered a mention of him in a letter by the lead Scotland Yard investigator for the murders, Chief Inspector John Littlechild.

Littlechild wrote that he believed "a very likely [suspect] ... was an American quack named Francis Tumblety ... his feelings toward women were remarkable and bitter in the extreme." Tumblety apparently kept a collection of uteri and had professed his hatred for women upon finding out that a former wife had been a prostitute.

The authors suggest that out of embarrassment at losing such a promising suspect, Scotland Yard buried the information, which the British press didn't cover at all and the American press mentioned only briefly.

For as much attention as Jack the Ripper has received over the years, the mysterious killer is only officially "credited" with five murders, starting with Mary Ann "Polly" Nichols' death on Buck Row—the shadiest part of London's Whitechapel—in August 1888. Murders continued until 1891 but were never officially linked with the Ripper—and they stopped when Tumblety fled across the pond.

The brutal nature of Jack the Ripper's crimes—hacking up the bodies of prostitutes—combined with the fact that he seemed to be able to slip in and out of the London fog unnoticed have made him legendary in the world of true crime.

And yet we're still not sure who he was.

Q: How did one murderer get away with selling victims' skeletons to medical students?

A: H.H. Holmes, the Torture Doctor, made murder into a business when he killed guests and employees at his Chicago hotel, The Castle, and then stripped the corpses of flesh and sold the skeletons to medical schools. The recipients never bothered to ask how the good doctor was obtaining so many skeletons.

This "enterprise" was an extension of an insurance scam that Holmes, born Herman W. Mudgett, had utilized to pay for his education at the University of Michigan, where he earned his medical degree. Holmes would obtain coverage for nonexistent people, disfigure stolen corpses, and then make insurance claims that the "insured" had been injured in accidents. Later he would use his "Murder Castle" in Chicago's Englewood neighborhood to create his own corpses—i.e., to kill.

When Holmes first moved to Chicago in the 1880s he bought a pharmacy from a woman who soon disappeared, and later he specially built a home/hotel across the street—all the while carrying out various swindles. One involved the sale of worthless "cures" for ailments, and in another he stiffed a furniture company for payment by building a wall around delivered items, avoiding repossession. Holmes then began taking advantage of the fact that many tourists, including young women, passed through his hotel during the 1893 World's Fair in Chicago—and they began disappearing.

Holmes' Castle was like a Hollywood house of horrors, with secret passageways among a confusing maze of hallways and staircases, soundproofed and windowless rooms, and a gas chamber. The rooms were equipped with trapdoors that dropped victims straight to the basement, which contained vats of acid, holes filled with quicklime, and a crematorium for disposing of bodies.

After the World's Fair ended, the doctor left Chicago and persuaded acquaintance Benjamin Pitzel (also reported as Pitezel) to take out a life insurance policy and fake his death to share the proceeds with Holmes. But Holmes killed Pitzel and used the actual corpse to claim the insurance money for himself. Unfortunately for Holmes, he had shared the original plot with a former jail companion, Marion Hedgepath, who ratted him out to authorities.

The exact number of Holmes' victims at Murder Castle is unknown, though it may be anywhere from nine to more than 200. Holmes—who famously said, "I was born with the devil in me"—confessed to 27 murders. After being tried for the murder of Pitzel, he was hanged in Philadelphia in 1896.

Q: Who told David Berkowitz to commit his heinous crimes, according to him?

A: David Berkowitz, aka the Son of Sam, told authorities that neighbor Sam Carr's black Labrador retriever, named Harvey, was possessed by demons and had urged him to murder for "the blood of pretty girls." The killer later admitted that the voices were a "silly hoax" that he never imagined would take on a life of its own.

Between July 1976 and July 1977, Berkowitz lurked in the shadows of New York City's boroughs with his .44 caliber Bulldog revolver. During that time he killed six people and wounded seven others.

Born Richard David Falco, Berkowitz was adopted by Bronx hardware store owners Nathan and Pearl Berkowitz, who switched the order of his first and middle names and attached their own surname. He was of above-average intelligence but didn't much care for school, preferring to explore his budding interest in pyromania. Some believe Berkowitz was pushed into murder by the discovery of the truth about his birth— that he was the product of an affair between his natural mother and her married lover, who wasn't interested in raising him.

Berkowitz says his violent streak started in 1975, when he stabbed a 15-year-old girl with a hunting knife in the Bronx. He moved to Yonkers shortly thereafter and graduated to using a gun. On July 29, 1976, Berkowitz claimed his first murder victim when he walked up to a parked car in the Bronx, pulled a pistol out of a paper bag, and fired several shots into the vehicle. Donna Lauria, 18, died instantly, while her friend Jody Valenti survived a bullet to her thigh.

Over the next year Berkowitz would take the lives of Christine Freund (age 26), Virginia Voskerichian (19), Alexander Esau (20), Valentina Suriani (18), and Stacy Moskowitz (20). He also shot Harvey the Labrador retriever (who recovered) and began sending strange letters to neighbors and former landlords.

Berkowitz was caught when an eyewitness saw something and said something. She remembered seeing a police officer ticket a car parked too close to a fire hydrant and, just after that, a man who freaked her out—followed by gunshots from behind. Investigators were able to track down Berkowitz's Ford Galaxie from her information. Once placed under arrest, Berkowitz confessed.

He flatly refused to plead not guilty by reason of insanity and instead pleaded guilty. Berkowitz's antics—including calling his last victim a "whore" in open court—made for bizarre proceedings and led the court to order yet another psychiatric evaluation, even after three mental health professionals had judged him legally sane to stand trial.

Since his conviction in 1978, Berkowitz has been denied parole twice and is still serving out six life sentences. He claims he has found God in prison and now calls himself the "Son of Hope."

Q: What is screen legend Peter Lorre's connection to serial killers? Hint: two-part answer.

A: Kenneth Bianchi and Angelo Buono, Jr.—jointly known as the Hillside Strangler—were cousins who posed as police officers to gain the trust of potential victims. One almost-victim was actor Peter Lorre's 24-year-old daughter Catharine, in 1977. Once the men realized who the young woman was, they quickly decided to let her go so as not to draw unwanted attention to themselves.

Lorre's other connection with serial killers is his professional portrayal of a serial killer who preyed upon young girls in the 1931 German film *M*.

Back to the Hillside Strangler. Let's start with the misleading name, which implies just one killer. The name was given to the unidentified murderer of 10 girls and young women, ages 12 to 28, in Los Angeles between October 1977 and February 1978. The Strangler was named for the method of death combined with the locations of the bodies.

Interestingly, Bianchi and Buono weren't cousins by blood. Bianchi was adopted by Buono's mother's sister and her husband. Prior to their Hillside Strangler days, Bianchi was into stealing jewelry from the store where he was a security guard, while Buono was already raping young girls—though neither had yet been caught for their crimes.

Bianchi hooked up with Buono in Los Angeles in 1977. After deciding to run a business as pimps, the cousins quickly discovered their common interest in rape and murder. As the deaths piled up, Bianchi applied to be a cop and even did some ride-alongs with the police department on searches for the Strangler.

Only after Bianchi—again with a job as a security guard—committed two additional murders in Bellingham, Washington, were police clued in to the identities and MO of the killers. In addition to posing as law enforcement and strangling their victims, this included sexual abuse and monstrous torture such electric shock, chemical injection, and carbon monoxide poisoning.

Once Bianchi was linked to the two Washington victims, the similarities with the Los Angeles cases became apparent. He eventually pleaded guilty and implicated his cousin to avoid the death penalty. Both men received sentences of life imprisonment. Buono died in 2002, while Bianchi is still serving his sentence in Washington.

Q: Who got the Boston Strangler off on homicide charges in exchange for pleading guilty to rape?

A: Attorney F. Lee Bailey is known for his deft handling of high-profile cases, and with Albert DeSalvo's he certainly got legal circles talking. Bailey counts among his past clients O. J. Simpson and Sam Sheppard, the neurosurgeon convicted and later exonerated of the murder of his wife—the inspiration for *The Fugitive* television show and movie.

DeSalvo's legally documented creepy history with women dates to 1960, when he confessed to being "The Measuring Man," a slick guy who weaseled his way into Boston-area apartments by telling women he was a modeling agent and then fondled them as he took their measurements. He served 11 months for assault and lewd conduct for that, but when he got out he dropped the ploy and simply started breaking into the homes of victims, raping and later murdering them.

The lawyer managed to finagle nary a murder charge for his client, who had confessed to being the Boston Strangler—the rapist and murderer of 13 women, ages 19 to 85, between 1962 and 1964. Note that DeSalvo didn't assault or strangle 85-year-old Mary Mullen, but her death is attributed to him because she had a heart attack when he broke into her home.

Instead of murder charges, DeSalvo only faced charges based on confessing to more than 2,000 rapes as "The Green Man"—so named because he wore green work clothes when he broke into his victims' homes.

As the Strangler, after raping his victims (sometimes with foreign objects), DeSalvo usually killed them by strangulation. Often he did so with their own pantyhose, which is why the crimes are sometimes called the "silk stockings murders." He would generally leave whatever was used for strangulation (sometimes a pillowcase, for instance) tied in a neat bow around the victim's neck. He also sometimes stabbed victims, and he left bite marks on the breast of one of the youngest victims.

DeSalvo received a sentence of life imprisonment but recanted his confession before he was stabbed to death in 1973 by a fellow inmate. Authorities questioned whether DeSalvo had actually killed the Strangler's supposed last victim, 19-year-old Mary Sullivan, because he claimed he had raped her, but the autopsy didn't reveal sexual activity. In 2013, however, detectives surreptitiously got a DNA sample from DeSalvo's nephew, using a discarded water bottle, and tests did link DeSalvo with the Sullivan murder.

Still, some believe that DeSalvo was not the killer of all the victims attributed to the Strangler. Perhaps there were two Stranglers, they say, one who focused on older women and one who targeted the younger ones. DeSalvo knew so many details about the crime scenes, they say, because he was fed the information by former fellow patient/inmate George Nassar at Bridgewater State Hospital. Nassar is also a convicted murderer, though he proclaims his innocence.

Bailey, incidentally, was disbarred in Florida in 2001 for attorney misconduct, including mishandling of client funds by mixing them with personal assets, *ex parte* communication with a judge, conflict of interest, self-dealing, and false testimony under oath. That led to reciprocal disbarment in Massachusetts, and Bailey hasn't been able to legally practice law since then.

Q: Who is the Co-Ed Killer who started at age 15 by killing his grandparents?

A: Edmund Kemper ranks quite high on the serial killer depravity scale, and that's saying something. He began by killing his paternal grandparents and didn't stop until he brought it all back to his family by murdering his alcoholic mother.

Even though Kemper eventually grew to 6'9" and 300-plus pounds, he was bullied relentlessly as a child. The constant harassment couldn't have helped the development of this intellectually gifted young boy; Kemper's IQ is in the "genius" range at 145. Unfortunately, Guy (as he was known) was already playing sexually charged games with his sister's dolls, decapitating them before moving on to torturing cats. Kemper buried one feline alive, dug it up, cut its head off, and mounted it as a trophy.

His mother, Clarnell Strandberg, called him "a real weirdo" and physically and emotionally abused him. She couldn't handle the young lad—imagine that—so she sent him to live with his grandparents on their farm in North Fork, California.

That ... didn't go well.

On August 27, 1964, Kemper shot his grandmother, who had been typing up the final draft of an article for *Boy's Life*, the Boy Scouts magazine. He took the .22 rifle he had received as a gift the previous Christmas, shot her in the back of the head and back, and then stabbed her three times because he didn't think she was dead and didn't want her to suffer. When his grandfather arrived home, Kemper shot and killed him, too. The boy said he was "mad at the world." He was placed in a psychiatric facility, where he was diagnosed with paranoid schizophrenia.

In May 1972, a few years after his release, Kemper began his pattern of picking up hitchhiking young women, killing them, decapitating them, and raping their corpses. Fresno State University students Mary Ann Pesce and Anita Luchessa were the first of Kemper's six co-ed victims. Between September 1972 and February 1973, Kemper also killed 15-year-old Aiko Koo, 19-year-old Cindy Schall, 24-year-old Rosalind Thorpe, and 21-year-old Alice Liu.

Kemper ended his serial killing career in April 1973 by bludgeoning his sleeping mother's head with a hammer, slitting her throat, cutting off her head, and raping her corpse. He then called over his mother's friend Sara Hallett to murder and decapitate her as well. On the run as police searched for the Co-Ed Killer, Kemper called from Pueblo, Colorado, to confess.

Although Kemper believed his appropriate punishment would be "death by torture," California had no death penalty at that time. And so he is serving a life term in prison. By all accounts he has been a model prisoner and has repeatedly waived his right to parole hearings. Perhaps, thankfully, that's his 145 IQ telling him he definitely should not be out among the rest of us.

Q: What serial killer was the inspiration for the Clint Eastwood film *Dirty Harry*?

A: The Zodiac Killer holds that honor. In the 1971 film, Inspector "Dirty" Harry Callahan pursues a psychopathic killer named Charles Davis who is fond of calling the police and sending them notes. The killer refers to himself as "Scorpio."

In real life, Zodiac is officially connected with the deaths of five people—though he claimed 37 victims. He taunted police by calling them and sending letters to the press with messages coded in cryptograms, in which he referred to himself as "Zodiac." He signed many of his letters with a crosshairs symbol and once said he would "wipe out a school bus" so he could "pick off the kiddies as they come bouncing out."

The identity of the real Zodiac Killer, however, remains unclear more than 50 years after he first struck in 1968. The first two victims officially recognized by authorities were 17-year-old David Faraday and 16-year-old Betty Lou Jensen, killed with a .22 pistol just before Christmas as they sat in a car at Lake Herman Road in Benicia, California.

Zodiac's next attack was on July 4, 1969. He approached the parked car of Darlene Ferrin, age 22, and Michael Mageau, 19, in the Blue Rock Springs Park parking lot in Vallejo, California. He shot them both, but Mageau survived.

After that shooting, Zodiac called the police to point them in the direction of the crime scene and let them know he had also "killed those kids last year." At the end of July, Zodiac sent letters to three newspapers claiming responsibility for the two attacks; each contained one-third of a cryptogram that Zodiac said would provide his identity if the code was cracked. A week later he sent another letter to the *San Francisco Examiner* including crime details that hadn't been made public.

Salinas schoolteacher Donald Harden and his wife Bettye solved the cryptogram soon after it was published. With its various spelling mistakes, the message conveyed that Zodiac found murdering people "so much fun" and a "most thrilling experience" that he preferred to "killing wild game in the forest."

At Lake Berryessa on September 27, 1969, donning a freaky square-topped hood with a white crosshairs painted on it, Zodiac tied up Bryan Hartnell, age 20, and Cecilia Ann Shepard, 22, and stabbed each of them several times. Before leaving the scene, he scribbled on Hartnell's car the dates of the previous killings along with the current date, noting "by knife." He called it the "double murder," though Hartnell survived.

The final Zodiac murder was on October 11 in San Francisco, when the serial killer shot taxi driver Paul Stine, 29, with a 9 mm semiautomatic pistol. A piece of Stine's bloody shirt later appeared with a letter sent by the Zodiac.

The lead suspect in the case is the late Arthur Leigh Allen, a convicted child molester from Vallejo. Surviving victim Mageau identified him as Zodiac, Allen's watch featured a crosshairs symbol, and his boots matched those worn by Zodiac. A friend of his who was interviewed by detectives said he had partially confessed.

Allen died in 1992, so he's not talking—and fingerprints, handwriting, and DNA analyses appear to exclude him as the perpetrator. And so the Zodiac mystery continues.

Q: Which serial killer was the inspiration for Alfred Hitchcock's film *Psycho*?

A: In his 1959 book *Psycho*, author Robert Bloch based the character of Norman Bates on Ed Gein. The novel became a film a year later. The connections are somewhat loose, but the incredible creepiness factor of both the real-life Gein and the fictional character is indisputable.

Gein's childhood featured an alcoholic father and a domineering mother with a strong belief that sex was evil. The family lived a rather isolated life on a Wisconsin farm, and Gein's mother wouldn't allow him or his brother to marry and leave the homestead. Within the span of five years in the 1940s, Gein lost his mother, father, and brother, leaving him alone. His brother Henry, who died in a forest fire, is believed by some to have been Gein's first victim, as no autopsy was performed.

Authorities were first drawn to Gein after 58-year-old Bernice Worden disappeared from her Plainfield hardware store. An incomplete bill of sale for antifreeze, made out to Gein, was found on the counter. Police discovered Worden's body in one of Gein's unlocked outbuildings, hanging from the ceiling and gutted like an animal. Her head was in a nearby sink, and her heart was in a pot on the stove.

And then there was the inside of his farmhouse with its collection of skulls (some used as bowls) and various fashion accessories crafted from body parts—including a suit made of human skin and bracelets of skin and hair. Gein confessed to the murder of a woman named Mary Hogan three years prior and admitted to robbing 40 or so graves so he could use body parts for decorating his desolate farmhouse and making costumes for himself.

Incidentally, he never dug up his mother like the fictional Norman Bates did, preferring simply to slip on his suit of human skin at night, put on his mother's clothes over it, and talk to her. Gein claimed he wanted a sex change operation to be closer to his dead mom, and indeed he was reportedly obsessed with the details of Christine Jorgensen's sex reassignment surgery in the early 1950s.

Bonus points if you are also reminded of Leatherface in *The Texas Chainsaw Massacre* or Buffalo Bill in *The Silence of the Lambs*. Those characters were also inspired by Gein's depravity.

Gein is suspected in several other murders as well, because some organs found at his house were never matched to known dead bodies, and also because two men had gone missing after visiting him.

Diagnosed as schizophrenic, Gein was declared mentally incompetent to stand trial and spent several months at Wisconsin's Central State Hospital for the Criminally Insane in Waupun in 1958. When he made it to trial he was found not guilty by reason of insanity. Gein lived out the rest of his days as a model patient, fashioning women's handbags from cloth and beads, until his death in 1984.

Film director John Waters, noted murderabilia collector, is reported to own Gein's death certificate.

Q: What killer was caught because he left a bloody footprint on his victim?

A: Richard Ramirez, the Night Stalker, left a print of his Avia sneaker when he kicked 61-year-old Joyce Lucille Nelson in the head. Avia prints were found at the scenes of several of the Night Stalker's murders.

On July 7, 1985, Ramirez found Nelson sleeping on her couch when he broke into her house in Monterey Park, California. He brutally beat her to death, and the kick to her head later helped nail Ramirez for his crimes.

Ramirez was a living nightmare, often taking advantage of open windows and unlocked doors to break into houses in Southern California as the occupants slept. If he found a couple, he would rape and/or sodomize the woman and murder the man; he usually also stole their jewelry. Ramirez killed 13 men and women between June 1984 and August 1985, terrorizing Los Angeles during the summer of 1985. By then, residents knew a serial killer was on the loose—leading to a spike in gun sales, according to a Northridge shop owner.

Ramirez either shot, beat, or stabbed victims so severely around the neck that some were nearly decapitated. He gouged out the eyes of one victim and put them in a jewelry box, which he then stole from the house. A Satanist, Ramirez drew pentagrams at some scenes and made some of the women "swear to Satan" that they wouldn't scream for help. He used a hammer to bludgeon one victim, a machete on another, and electric shocks for yet another.

At the end of August police located Ramirez's car, thanks to eyewitnesses, and were able to lift a print that identified him as their man. With Ramirez's mug shots plastered everywhere, the killer picked the wrong neighborhood when he went to East LA to try to steal the car of Angelina de la Torre. She screamed, and an angry mob converged on Ramirez, chasing him down and beating him with baseball bats and tire irons until police officers arrived.

After his arrest, deputies heard Ramirez humming AC/DC's "Night Prowler" and later watched him dip a finger into his bloodied palm and scrawl "666" on the floor of his holding cell. His bizarre bursts of laughter peppered his trial, which took four years and cost $1.6 million. He was convicted of 13 murders and 30 other felonies and was sentenced to death.

Ramirez sat on California's death row for 23 years before dying of natural causes in 2013.

Q: Which serial killer shares the name of one of Elaine's boyfriends on TV's Seinfeld?

A: In the *Seinfeld* episode called "The Masseuse," Elaine Benes is dating Joel Rifkin, and many jokes are made about his sharing a name with serial killer Joel Rifkin—notorious as the Long Island Killer. At a New York Giants football game, chaos ensues when Rifkin's name is announced over the P.A. system, and even linebacker Lawrence Taylor raises an eyebrow—causing fictional Joel to decide it's time to change his name. The actual Rifkin's 71-year-old mother was reportedly quite upset by the episode, which aired only five months after her son's arrest and before he had gone to trial.

In 1989 the real Joel Rifkin went from visiting prostitutes to killing Heidi Balch, whom he had brought to his family's Long Island home when his mother and sister were out of town. After bludgeoning, suffocating, and strangling Balch, he went to sleep; six hours later he began to decapitate and dismember her body with an X-Acto knife. He also removed her teeth and scraped off her fingerprints to make identification difficult. Rifkin scattered Balch's body parts throughout Long Island, New Jersey, and New York City.

About 16 months later his mother and sister left town again, and Rifkin brought a prostitute named Julia Blackbird to the house. He beat and strangled her, then placed her remains in buckets, poured concrete around them, and dumped the buckets into the East River and the Brooklyn Canal.

Over the next three years Rifkin killed another 15 women in similar fashion—after having sex with them, he strangled them—though his disposal methods differed slightly. For one stretch, for instance, he placed his victims' bodies in oil drums and dumped them into various bodies of water.

Then, in the middle of the night on June 28, 1993, Rifkin was transporting the body of his last victim, 22-year-old Tiffany Bresciani, when police officers noticed that his pickup had no tags. They tried to pull him over but Rifkin wouldn't stop, which eventually led to his slamming into a utility pole. The stench of the decomposing body in his vehicle gave him away immediately.

Rifkin confessed to 17 murders, and a search of his house revealed his victims' clothing, driver's licenses, purses, and more. A vial of human blood and a chainsaw with human blood and flesh stuck in the blades were found in the garage. A bumper sticker on one of his vehicles read, "Sticks and stones may break my bones, but whips and chains excite me."

On the murder of Bresciani, Rifkin declined a plea deal of 46 years to life because he wanted to take his chances on an insanity plea. It didn't work. He was found guilty of that murder and eight others over the course of several trials. He was sentenced to 203 years total in prison.

Q: Ted Bundy was consulted on the case of a fellow killer. Which one?

A: Washington state authorities sometimes met with convicted serial killer Ted Bundy to discuss the possible movements of the Green River Killer. One piece of advice Bundy gave investigators was to stake out a recent victim's burial site, because the killer probably returned to have sex with corpses. Apparently it really does take one to know one, because Bundy was right about Gary Ridgway.

The Green River Killer murdered as many as 71 women between 1982 and 1998. He got his nickname because he disposed of most of the bodies—invariably nude—near the Green River in Washington. Although the highly religious Ridgway spoke out against prostitutes cluttering the area, he used their services often, and many became his victims.

Ridgway's MO was to flash a photo of his son to appear innocuous. After the prostitute went with him to a secluded place—usually his truck or house—he raped and strangled her.

Ridgway's penchant for prostitutes helped authorities catch him, because once they began looking into people with prostitution-related convictions, Ridgway was firmly on their radar. The killer managed to pass a polygraph test in 1984 but couldn't escape DNA evidence. In 1987 police took hair and saliva samples from him after a search warrant carried out on his property and vehicles turned up no evidence, even though authorities suspected Ridgway was the Green River Killer. Technology wasn't advanced enough in the late 80s to place Ridgway at any murder scenes, but by 2001 it was. He was initially linked to four victims.

When all was said and done, Ridgway pled guilty to 48 murders and received a total sentence of 480 years in prison, with no chance of parole.

Q: What pint-sized killer has been called a "redneck Charlie Manson"?

A: Donald "Pee Wee" Gaskins was one of the worst serial killers in South Carolina history. He was convicted of 10 murders, and his victims included a two-year-old girl, her pregnant mother, and three teens—including his own 15-year-old niece. He claimed to have killed far more people than that, however, with the body count potentially reaching 100 or more.

Gaskins was reportedly somewhere between 5'2" and 5'5" tall, but what he lacked in stature, he compensated for in cruelty. Most of his victims were hitchhikers—both male and female—that he shot, stabbed, beat, strangled, drowned, raped, sodomized, mutilated, and in some cases even cannibalized. When it came time to bury them, he transported them in his purple hearse.

Unsurprisingly, Gaskins didn't hang around with a high caliber of folk, and one of his criminal acquaintances sold him out to police in 1975 for killing Dennis Beegee Bellamy and Johnny Knight. He confessed— he even showed police where more bodies were buried—and was sentenced to death after being convicted on several murder counts.

Another death sentence came with the 1977 trial for the contract murder of wealthy farmer Silas Barnwell Yates, whose girlfriend Suzanne Kipper Owens hired Gaskins for the killing. The diminutive serial killer wouldn't admit to that murder, though he readily admitted to nine others. Word of Gaskins' plan to write a book about his life didn't go over well; the prosecutor said Gaskins' additional confessions were false, and his way of creating "sensational headlines, for his book."

Gaskins' death sentence was commuted to life imprisonment when South Carolina laws changed regarding the death penalty. But then he went and got himself a death sentence back by killing a fellow death row inmate in 1982. Gaskins killed Rudolph Tyner by delivering him a radio with a homemade bomb inside.

Just before his scheduled execution, Gaskins attempted suicide by slashing his arms with a razor blade he had swallowed a week before—this despite the fact that he was under 24-hour watch by six guards. His date with the electric chair went ahead as planned, and Gaskins died on September 6, 1991.

Q: Who was England's Dr. Death, convicted of murdering 15 patients by lethal injection?

A: Harold Shipman was a throwback to old-fashioned doctors—hands-on and fond of making house calls. He was also the most prolific serial killer in British history.

"Virtually every family and every street" of Hyde, Cheshire, England was touched by the murders of Shipman, according to *The Telegraph*, and that hardly seems an exaggeration. Authorities believe the family doctor may have killed as many as 250 of his patients. A local Roman Catholic priest who aided in the exhumations of six Shipman victims said he wouldn't be surprised if the actual number is closer to 500.

Had anyone been paying closer attention, the murders might have stopped long before Shipman was arrested in 1998 after a local funeral home and the coroner raised concerns. At the same time, the will of Kathleen Grundy, 81, was coming under scrutiny because she had left a large chunk of money to Shipman but nothing to her immediate family.

When investigators looked at 15 recent cases for which Shipman had signed death certificates, they found that he had administered diamorphine (heroin used for pain management), signed the certificates without consulting with colleagues, and falsified records to state that the patients had been doing poorly. Many of his patients (mostly elderly women) expired around the same time in the middle of the afternoon. A search of Shipman's property revealed the typewriter that had been used to draw up Grundy's suspicious will. Extensive investigation revealed that Shipman's murders dated back to 1974.

Shipman was convicted of 15 murders committed between 1995 and 1998 and sentenced to life imprisonment without parole, but his prison time was ended by his own hand in 2004 when he used his bed sheets to hang himself. He had denied responsibility for the deaths and refused to speak about them. Accordingly, no motive was ever discerned. The only time he attempted to profit financially was with Grundy's will, which was what ended up getting him caught.

Some surmise that Shipman relished the feeling of being in complete control of life and death, but British Health Secretary Alan Milburn put it quite succinctly: "Harold Shipman was a cold, calculating, evil killer."

Q: Who managed to keep murdering even after police placed a tracking device on his car?

A: Carl "Coral" Watts, the Sunday Morning Slasher, terrorized women in Texas, Michigan, and even Ontario, Canada, from the mid-1970s until his arrest in 1982. In all, he killed between 22 and 100 women and injured another 40 or so. Watts kidnapped victims from their homes and tortured them in various ways before murdering them.

He proved difficult for authorities to nail down because he moved across jurisdictions, changed his methods of killing—bludgeoning, drowning, strangling, stabbing—and usually didn't sexually assault his victims. That made even trace DNA difficult to gather at a time when forensic testing was still in its infancy.

Still, Watts was on police radar for years before he was ultimately arrested in Texas in 1982. Detective Paul Bunten in Ann Arbor, Michigan, was an especially dogged pursuer of Watts, and his work ultimately led to keeping the Slasher behind bars. Based on a tip from a Detroit police officer that Watts—who had a history of mental hospital stays and violence against women—was a suspect in killings in Kalamazoo, Bunten began surveillance on Watts.

One night in November 1980, two police officers saw Watts become upset after losing a stalking target, and they arrested him for driving with a suspended license. Bunten interviewed Watts, but when questioning veered toward unsolved murders, Watts stopped talking and asked for a lawyer. The detective was convinced he had a killer in front of him but couldn't prove it. The hunt was on, and the following week Bunten secured a court order to track Watts' car.

The Ann Arbor killings stopped, but Bunten kept watching as Watts moved throughout Michigan and into Ontario and back. He even got Watts back in for more questioning after searching his apartment, but then Watts disappeared in March 1981. He turned up in Texas, which Bunten found out from talking with Watts' coworkers and then informed Houston police.

Unfortunately, Watts managed to kill over and over again before cops were able to nab him. Then on May 23, 1982, Watts was dragging Lori Lister into her Houston apartment after choking her unconscious when he ran into Lister's roommate, Melinda Aguilar. Watts tied Aguilar's wrists but she escaped, and police were able to chase down Watts.

Even in Texas, prosecutors feared they didn't have enough evidence to secure a conviction, so they made a unique—some might argue ill-advised—plea deal with him. The state would forego murder charges if Watts would plead guilty to burglary with the intent to murder—a 60-year sentence—and help them clear the books on the Texas murders he did commit. Watts accepted and gave details on 13 homicides.

Things got procedurally complicated when Watts remained eligible for parole and Texas scheduled his release for 2006. Re-enter Michigan authorities, who refused to let Watts get away with murder. The Michigan Attorney General publicly requested that anyone with information in the 1979 killing of 36-year-old Helen Dutcher come forward, and Joseph Foy did. He identified Watts as the person he saw kill Dutcher, and Watts was convicted and sentenced to life imprisonment without parole.

The Sunday Slasher died of prostate cancer in prison in 2007, finally ending the Slasher saga some 30 years after it began.

Q: How did investigators finally zero in on the Golden State Killer?

A: In 2018 police arrested 72-year-old Joseph James DeAngelo on suspicion of being the Golden State Killer (GSK), alternately known as the East Area Rapist or East Bay Rapist, Original Night Stalker, Visalia Ransacker, and Diamond Knot Killer. Investigators arrived at their conclusion through a DNA match in a genealogy database.

Months before, lead detective Paul Holes had uploaded the DNA from one of the rape kits connected to GSK to the GEDmatch website, which identified enough distant relatives to develop a family tree. From there, investigators were led to two suspects; one was ruled out by subsequent DNA testing—and that left DeAngelo.

Authorities maintain that DeAngelo is linked to more than a dozen murders and 50 rapes from 1976 through 1986 in California, between Sacramento and Orange County. Three separate crime sprees seemed distinct at first, but as DNA technology became more advanced, police were able to link them.

GSK stalked his victims to determine their movements and then pounced in the dark of night, slipping in and out of open gates and windows without being detected even by neighbors' dogs. He would shine a flashlight in his victims' faces to disorient them, rape the woman in a sleeping couple, and then kill both man and woman. He enjoyed taunting police and even survivors of his attacks with phone calls. In 2001, GSK called a woman to ask, "Remember when we played?"—24 years after he had assaulted her.

True crime author Michelle McNamara's 2018 book *Into the Dark* is widely credited with keeping the GSK case in the spotlight. Police had announced a renewed effort to capture him in 2016 as McNamara was shoulders-deep in her research.

DeAngelo's court case is ongoing. The six California counties in which GSK allegedly committed felonies have agreed to work together, and DeAngelo currently faces 13 counts of murder and another 13 charges on rape-related offenses. Reports estimate that his trial could take a decade or more and cost taxpayers $20 million.

Meanwhile, "genetic genealogy" appears poised to take over a central role in solving cold cases.

Q: What technology-related evidence helped bring nurse Charles Cullen to justice?

A: His browsing history is what caught up with him.

Amy Loughren, an astute coworker of Cullen's, went snooping around his computer activity to see what he'd been doing instead of charting. What she found led her to believe it was her friend Charlie who had been killing off patients at Somerset Medical Center in New Jersey.

Loughren noticed that Cullen had been accessing the medical records of patients who weren't his own, and she worked with the police as an informant. As it turned out, Cullen was preparing IV bags with lethal drug cocktails for fellow nurses to deliver to their patients, thereby distancing himself from the crimes. He followed the progress of how the drugs were affecting the patients on their charts, as if he were watching NCAA basketball tournament results.

Cullen had also figured out how to rig the machine that dispensed medicine so he could request one type and receive another.

His scheme was almost revealed when several patients went into insulin shock at St. Barnabas Hospital in Livingston, New Jersey. Cullen had been contaminating IV bags, and although there was an internal investigation, no state authorities were notified and Cullen simply switched jobs. In fact, he bounced around among many hospitals in Pennsylvania and New Jersey over the course of his nursing career, killing patients along the way.

After his arrest in 2003 Cullen confessed to 40 murders, but estimates on the actual total reach more than 300. He received multiple life sentences after pleading guilty to 29 murders in New Jersey and more in Pennsylvania. Cullen's crimes led New Jersey to pass the Patient Safety Act, which facilitates the sharing of employee-related information among health care facilities.

Ironically, from prison Cullen saved a life in 2006 when he donated one of his kidneys to the brother of an ex-girlfriend to "atone for his sins."

Q: Who is known as the Atlanta Child Killer despite not being charged with killing any children?

A: The Wayne Williams case is an intriguing one for true crime buffs, as his characterization as the Atlanta Child Killer barely passes the smell test. Even renowned FBI profiler John Douglas, who worked on the case in the early 1980s, doesn't believe Williams committed all 23 of the murders attributed to him, though he does maintain that Williams is guilty of some.

"We have an idea who did some of the others," Douglas wrote in his book *Mindhunter*. "It isn't a single offender and the truth isn't pleasant."

The Atlanta child murders refer to a series of deaths of young black boys, ages seven to 17, between 1979 and 1981. Williams became the lead suspect when he was spotted on a bridge in May of 1981 just as there was a splash in the water below. The body of convicted felon Nathaniel Cater, age 27, was found in the river three days later. Even though eyewitness testimony suggested Cater was alive days after the splash, Williams was convicted of his murder.

At trial, the prosecution offered fiber evidence linking Williams' vehicles and home to some of the victims, but he was never charged or prosecuted for the murders of any children. Instead, Williams was convicted for Cater's death and for the murder of 21-year-old Jimmy Ray Payne. Atlanta called off the investigation of the "child murders" soon after. Williams was sentenced to two consecutive life terms.

A declassified Georgia Bureau of Investigation report suggests that another explanation for the child murders is that the Ku Klux Klan was behind them, with the intention of starting a race war. Klan member Charles Sander allegedly bragged that he had murdered one of the young boys on the "List" after the boy rammed his car with a go-cart.

Still, questions remain in many minds. DeKalb County reopened and then reclosed four of the cases in the mid-2000s, and in March 2019, Atlanta Mayor Keisha Lance Bottoms announced the city's renewed efforts to identify the child killer once and for all.

Williams remains in prison in Georgia.

Q: Who is Florida's Classified Ad Rapist?

A: Bobby Joe Long turned to murder in Tampa in 1984 after raping more than 50 women in the Miami–Fort Lauderdale area.

Long scoured classified ads and visited the homes of women who would likely be alone, then raped and robbed them. He was convicted of rape in the early 1980s, but the charges were dropped after an appeal.

He wasn't that lucky when he was arrested for murder.

In November 1984, a brave young woman named Lisa McVey proved to be Long's downfall. Long abducted 17-year-old McVey and held her hostage at gunpoint in his apartment for 26 hours, repeatedly raping her. Despite being blindfolded, she managed to glimpse the make of Long's car—a red Dodge Magnum—and memorized details of his face by feeling it with her hands. She also purposely left fingerprints everywhere she could in his bathroom.

After Long told her he was assaulting her to get back at all women because of a bad breakup, McVey realized she needed to gain his trust to stay alive, so she pretended to want to be his girlfriend. Long didn't go for that, but he did agree to drop her off near where she lived— alive. Police arrested him a few weeks later and ended up linking him to several murders through fibers from his Magnum. McVey later became a sheriff's deputy.

Long, who called women "sluts," targeted prostitutes and exotic dancers ranging in age from 17 to 28. He bound his victims before either bludgeoning or stabbing them or slitting their throats, then left their bodies splayed in degrading positions by roadsides or in the woods. His eight-month killing bout claimed at least 10 victims.

Long's defense attorney, the flamboyant Ellis Rubin, tried several avenues for explaining Long's crimes during his trial for the murder of 22-year-old Michelle Denise Simms: his difficult childhood (including bullying thanks to the extra X chromosome that gave Long female-like breasts), several serious head injuries, a pornography addiction, drug use, and even violent video games. He argued that Long was a "special breed" whose depravity should be studied, not extinguished in the electric chair.

The jury didn't bite and sentenced Long to death. He remains on death row in Florida.

Q: How did Jerry Brudos commit murders at home without his wife knowing?

A: Brudos—alternately called the Lust Killer and the Shoe Fetish Slayer—simply told his wife, Ralphene, that she couldn't enter the garage of their Salem, Oregon, home without his permission. He said he was developing photographs and didn't want any light getting in. Since he was an electrician, it wasn't difficult for him to install an intercom system so she could call him when dinner was ready. She didn't even suspect anything when he moved the stand-alone freezer into the garage.

Brudos had been stealing and wearing women's underwear and shoes for years—reportedly since he was a small child—before he decided to procure personal models. His first victim was Linda Slawson, an encyclopedia-selling 23-year-old. He got her into his basement, where he hit her over the head with a plank, choked her, and dressed her corpse to his liking. He also cut off her left foot so he could use it in his chosen shoes. (Later he would cut off a victim's breast and preserve it in resin for use as a paperweight.) Then he tied an engine block to Slawson's body and dumped it into the Willamette River.

The garage quickly became Brudos' work space of choice, though, and he carried out the murders of three other young women there: Jan Susan Whitney (age 23), Linda Dawn Salee (22), and Karen Elena Sprinker (19). Brudos began having sex with their dead bodies and also took photographs of himself with the dressed and posed corpses; the photos were found in a police search of his home. After 34 years on death row, Long died by lethal injection on May 23, 2019, as victim Lisa McVey Noland watched.

Brudos almost got caught when he left Whitney's body in the garage and the family went away for the weekend. Someone crashed a car into his "work space," but the horrors inside weren't exposed.

Accounts of what led to Brudos' arrest are varied, but one interesting version recounts that when investigators interviewed University of Oregon students, they learned that a man was cold-calling young women to ask for blind dates. As it turned out, Brudos had been contacting the school and asking for the numbers of students with common names; then he would ask them to meet him for coffee. When detectives found a girl who had met with the mystery man who talked incessantly about the recently murdered local women, they asked her to let them know if he called again. He did, and police tracked down Brudos.

Brudos was eventually arrested for the attempted abduction of a 15-year-old girl, who was able to identify him. He confessed to the murders and received three life sentences in the Oregon State Penitentiary, where he died of liver cancer in 2006.

Somewhat lost in serial killer history is the fact that Brudos' wife, Ralphene, also faced first-degree murder charges in the death of Karen Sprinker. She was acquitted, divorced her husband, and got a court order forbidding him to see their two children.

Q: What true crime television show host lost a son to a serial killer?

A: John Walsh, host of *America's Most Wanted* and *In Pursuit with John Walsh*, lost his son Adam in 1981 when Adam was abducted from a Sears store in a Hollywood, Florida, shopping mall. Adam's severed head was recovered two weeks later in a drainage ditch in Indian River County.

Although no one ever faced charges in Adam's death, in 1983 Ottis Toole, partner-in-crime of fellow serial killer Henry Lee Lucas, confessed to the murder along with Lucas. Police were convinced that Toole was the perpetrator, because he knew details only the killer could know, but they also realized that Lucas couldn't have been involved as he had an alibi. That wasn't a problem for Toole as he simply changed his story about how it all went down but still accepted responsibility. And then he recanted. And then he confessed again. And recanted. Rinse and repeat, many times over.

Florida prosecutors never could pin down Toole for the Walsh murder, but they did manage to secure convictions for the murders of 64-year-old George Sonnenberg and 19-year-old Ada Johnson, each of which carried a death sentence.

In 1996, just as detectives were opening the books again on the Walsh case, Toole died of cirrhosis. Further complicating matters was the fact that every bit of DNA evidence from the Walsh murder was gone. John Walsh publicly called the Hollywood Police Department "incompetent," though detectives did continue to look into the case.

Jeffrey Dahmer was floated as a potential suspect for a while, but he denied any involvement.

Though no more evidence was ever found one way or the other, police announced the case closed and said that Toole was the killer who had taken Adam Walsh's life—which is what his father had long believed.

Q: Where did the DC Snipers' three-week murder spree begin in October 2002?

A: It all started in the parking lot of a Michaels craft store in Aspen Hill, Maryland—and rather ironically, the first shot didn't hit anyone. Less than an hour later, however, a 55-year-old man named James Martin was shot and killed in a parking lot in Wheaton, Maryland. By the time they were arrested, 41-year-old John Allen Muhammad and 17-year-old Lee Boyd (John Lee) Malvo had killed 10 people and injured another three—and inflicted terror on thousands in and around the nation's capital.

The random way the killers selected their victims made their crimes especially terrifying. Authorities could see no pattern regarding race, sex, or anything else, causing a veritable panic in the Beltway area and along Interstate 95 in Virginia.

Investigators linked Muhammad through a fingerprint found at an Alabama crime scene after a sniper hotline caller claimed responsibility for a September 2002 shooting in Montgomery, and Maryland police went on the hunt for him. Muhammad's second wife had obtained a permanent restraining order against him in 2000, and possession of a firearm was a violation.

The murderous duo was arrested at a Maryland rest stop. Police discovered they had cut a hole in the trunk of their dark blue Chevrolet Caprice through which a gun could be fired.

As the elder, Muhammad was undoubtedly the more dominant of the pair, but the motive for the shootings was never firmly established. One theory is that Muhammad was expressing anti-American sentiment as he sympathized with the September 11 terrorists, having converted to Islam in the mid-1980s. Muhammad was also prepared to request $10 million ransom from the US government to stop the shootings.

In 2003 Muhammad was convicted of shooting Dean Meyers at a gas station in Manassas, Virginia, along with related felonies. He was sentenced to death and executed in 2009.

Malvo is currently serving multiple life sentences, but in March 2019 the US Supreme Court decided to hear his appeal for a lesser sentence based on a 2012 ruling that mandatory life sentences without the possibility of parole for juveniles are unconstitutional in most cases—and that the provision should be applied retroactively. The case is expected to be heard in the fall of 2019.

Q: What nickname was serial killer Albert Fish given at the orphanage where he grew up?

A: Children at the orphanage called him Ham & Eggs. Partly to avoid that, he chose to go by the name of his deceased sibling Albert rather than use his given name, Hamilton.

St. John's Orphanage in Washington, DC, was scarring for young Fish for more than just a silly nickname. He was beaten—which he reportedly began to enjoy—and witnessed both physical and sexual abuse of other boys. He soon got together with a boy who taught him the finer points of such activities as eating feces and drinking urine, which became sexual fetishes for Fish.

His killing is believed to have started when Fish was 54, with the 1924 murder of eight-year-old Francis X. McDonnell. Fish sexually assaulted, strangled, and hung McDonnell from a tree.

His next confirmed victim was four-year-old Billy Gaffney, in 1927. Fish kidnapped him and tied him up, leaving him overnight and then whipping him the next day before he began mutilating the poor boy—cutting off his nose and ears and slicing his mouth from ear to ear. He also poked his eyeballs out. After the boy was dead, Fish pierced his stomach and drank his blood.

Grace Budd was the last of Fish's three known victims. Ten years old when Fish attacked her in 1928, she was strangled and dismembered, and then Fish took her body home in smaller pieces to eat the parts. He famously and disgustingly sent a ghastly and vulgar letter to

Grace's mother detailing how he had killed and eaten her daughter over nine days.

"How sweet and tender her little ass was roasted in the oven," he wrote.

Psychiatrists at Fish's trial testified that he had a host of fetishes, including sadism, masochism, and pedophilia—although for what it's worth, Fish did tell Grace's mother (in much more graphic language) that he hadn't violated her. Fish also engaged in self-mutilation; an X-ray introduced at his trial showed that he had inserted 12 needles into his groin.

Fish was also suspected in the deaths of five other children but was never definitively linked to those crimes.

Fish pleaded insanity, insisting that God had told him to kill the children. Though some jurors did think he was insane, they found the opposite, because they felt he should die regardless. Seated in the electric chair, Fish assisted the executioner in placing the electrodes on his body. His last words reportedly were "I don't even know why I'm here."

Q: Who was the Freeway Killer who played bridge with fellow serial killers on death row?

A: William Bonin was a two-time paroled sex offender before he became the sadistic leader of a murder ring in 1979 and 1980—and he was also the bridge partner of serial killers Lawrence Bittaker, Randy Kraft, and Douglas Clark as they awaited their executions.

Bonin confessed to 21 murders, though he was convicted of just 14, and authorities have linked him to 44 deaths. His victims were male prostitutes, hitchhikers, and other transients—always boys or young men. He would force or lure them into his Ford Econoline van and then restrain, rape, and beat them around the head and genitals. Bonin loved to hear their screams, an accomplice later said, so he would torture them before finally killing them—usually either by strangulation or stabbing. He forced one victim to drink hydrochloric acid and used an ice pick on another.

Bonin dumped the bodies of his victims along Southern California highways, a practice that the judge at his trial called "a gross, revolting affront to human dignity."

Along the way, Bonin picked up accomplices Vernon Butts, Gregory Miley, James Michael Munro, and William Ray Pugh, the last of whom would lead to his arrest. Pugh was being held for stealing a car when he started telling police about Bonin and his crimes. Based on Pugh's contentions, authorities placed Bonin under surveillance and caught him in the process of trying to rape a young boy in his van.

His accomplices were captured and faced various fates in the criminal justice system, mostly lengthy prison terms. Pugh, however, received just six years on a voluntary manslaughter charge and served only four before being released. Butts died by suicide before his trial, and Miley succumbed to injuries inflicted by another inmate in 2016.

Bonin's final claim to "fame"? He was the first person to die by lethal injection in California. He was executed in 1996.

Q: Who fashioned his RV into a torture chamber dubbed the Toy Box?

A: Suspected serial killer David Parker Ray, aka the Toy Box Killer, set up various pain-inflicting devices and mechanisms—including surgical tools, saws, whips, chains, leg spreaders, and pulleys—inside his soundproofed trailer near Elephant Butte, New Mexico. The trailer was also equipped with a gynecologist's table wired to give electric shocks.

Ray's RV of horrors was discovered when Cynthia Vigil escaped on March 22, 1999, after being tortured for two and a half to three days. Naked and wearing a metal collar and chains, she managed to free herself after a struggle with Ray's girlfriend, Cindy Hendy. Vigil broke down on the stand during Ray's trial when the prosecution asked her to identify the items she was found wearing upon her escape. She testified that Hendy had told her she'd "only been kidnapping, raping, and murdering girls for the past year," while Ray had been doing it for much longer. Vigil managed to stab Hendy in the neck with an ice pick to get out.

After Cindy's story was made public, another victim spoke up. Angelica Montano reported a similar story and said she had even told police, but nothing was ever done.

Authorities tracked down a third victim from a video they found among Ray's possessions. Kelli Garrett's tattooed ankle led law enforcement to her door to question her, and she confirmed that she, too, had been brutally tortured by Ray. The killer left her for dead on the side of the road, but she lived to tell her story—albeit several years later because, once again, no one had believed her at the time.

Ray kept a diary in which he wrote about his victims, which is why authorities place the number of potential victims between 40 and 60. After abducting or luring them to his trailer, he would keep them for days, even weeks, and torture them by various methods. He drugged them so they wouldn't be able to remember details to report the crimes, but most of his victims apparently ended up in nearby abandoned mines.

Ray pleaded guilty to rape and kidnapping charges and received a 223-year sentence but was never convicted of murder—and no victims' bodies were ever found. Hendy received a 36-year sentence, and as of 2018 she was being scheduled for release. Another accomplice, Dennis Yancy, was convicted of murdering his ex-girlfriend with Ray's help and was sentenced to two 15-year terms. Gloria Jean "Jesse" Ray, Ray's daughter, was sentenced to nine years in prison for her involvement.

Ray died of a heart attack in 2002.

Q: What "Alphabet" killer in California kept a to-do list of women to kill?

A: Crazy Joe Naso's murder list was found during a search of his home by parole authorities following up on a lead that he was trying to buy a gun and had two rounds of ammunition in his possession—both violations of his parole on a previous theft conviction.

Along with the list, authorities found hundreds of photographs of naked women who appeared to be either dead or unconscious, plus writings dating back to the 1950s detailing how he planned to attack other women, as well as descriptions and locations of his victims.

During closing arguments at Naso's 2013 trial for the murder of four women, Deputy District Attorney Rosemary Slote read bits of his diaries into the record : "Kansas City girl. Great legs in nylons, heels. Had to rape her in my car on a cold winter night, snowstorm."

A self-employed photographer and lifetime expert in petty crime, Naso killed six to 10 women in Northern California from 1977 to 1994. Four of his victims had matching initials—Roxene Roggasch, Carmen Colon, Pamela Parsons, and Tracy Tafoya—which led investigators to call the killings the Alphabet or Double Initial murders.

Naso would isolate his victims, often by kidnapping them, then strangle them and take their bodies to a rural area to dump them. Some women were also sexually assaulted.

When Roggasch's body was found, she was wearing only inside-out pantyhose. One pair of stockings was wrapped around her neck, another pair around her mouth, and a third pair shoved into her mouth. The pantyhose from her neck contained DNA from Naso's ex-wife, Judith. The crotch of the pantyhose Roggasch was wearing contained semen linked to Naso through DNA testing.

Because of a similarly themed stretch of killings in Rochester, New York—one of the child victims there, Carmen Colon, even had the same name as one of Naso's adult victims—Crazy Joe was also a suspect in those murders. Naso was a native of Rochester and traveled frequently between the two places, but DNA evidence eventually excluded him as a suspect.

Naso, who was 79 years old at the time of his trial, proclaimed his innocence and represented himself. But Crazy Joe was convicted on all four counts of murder, and in his final statement to the courtroom he flashed the middle finger to spectators. He was given the death penalty and remains on death row at California's San Quentin State Prison.

Q: What did Sunset Strip Killer Doug Clark do with the head of one victim?

A: Like several of his serial killing counterparts, Clark practiced necrophilia—having sexual relations or an attraction to corpses, or part of them. The head was Clark's favorite part.

Clark and his girlfriend and partner-in-crime, Carol Bundy, met in a Southern California bar in January 1980 and soon realized they shared similar interests—especially regarding murder and pedophilia. In the beginning of June of that year Clark killed 17-year-old Marnette Comer and then, on June 11, abducted two teenage girls, forced them to perform oral sex on him, shot them, raped their corpses, and left their bodies near the Ventura Freeway.

Karen Jones, 24, and Exxie Wilson, 20, were the pair's next two victims. On June 24, Wilson was decapitated, and her head was kept in the refrigerator. Bundy would apply makeup to it, and Clark used it for his necrophiliac activities.

At this point Bundy went rogue and confided about the crimes to a man she was getting interested in, Jack Robert Murray. Feeling that he was going to go to the police, however, she killed and decapitated him. But she couldn't live with the guilt and told a coworker, who reported the murder to the authorities.

Bundy spilled all the deets to the police, and to avoid the death penalty she accepted a plea bargain for a life sentence. Clark tried to pin everything on her but was convicted and sentenced to death in 1983.

Bundy died of heart failure in prison in 2003, while Clark still waits on death row.

Q: How did the Happy Face Killer get his name?

A: In the mid-1990s, *The Oregonian* columnist Phil Stanford wrote a series of articles about an unidentified killer who had sent a letter to the Portland newspaper confessing to crimes and had signed it with a happy face. Stanford referred to the murderer as the Happy Face Killer.

And what a story it is.

Taking advantage of his career as a long-haul truck driver, Keith Hunter Jesperson killed and disposed of his victims' remains across several states, enabling him to evade capture for years. His efforts at concealing his crimes were beyond gruesome, however, in the case of 21-year-old Angela Subrize. He tied her body face down to the underside of his truck and then drove at high speed for about 10 miles in an effort to make her unidentifiable.

Jesperson, a big guy at 6'8" and 240 pounds, easily overpowered his eight known victims in California, Florida, Nebraska, Oregon, Washington, and Wyoming between 1990 and 1995. Note that he claims the actual number of victims is approximately 160. He targeted sex workers and hitchhikers and usually raped and strangled them before tossing their bodies somewhere along his route.

His desire to lay claim to his crimes via anonymous confessions arose after the body of Taunja Bennett, his first victim, was discovered in a ditch in Portland and a woman named Laverne Pavlinac implicated herself and boyfriend John Sosnovske in the murder. Pavlinac later said that she had done so in an effort to get away from the abusive Sosnovske, figuring that getting him put in prison would do the trick. Pavlinac had done her homework on the case, because she managed to get them both convicted of the murder in 1991 even though they had nothing to do with it.

Jesperson wasn't fond of someone else taking credit for his criminality, so after Pavlinac's "confession" he wrote his own on a bus station bathroom wall in Livingston, Montana.

"I beat her to death, raped her and loved it," he wrote about Bennett. "Yes, I'm sick, but I enjoy myself too. People took the blame and I'm free." He signed it with a smiley face.

Jesperson wrote a similar confession a few days later in a bathroom in Umatilla, Oregon, again signing with a smiley face. Then years later he sent anonymous confessions to law enforcement and *The Oregonian*—always with his trademark smiley.

The postscript on Jesperson is that his last murder led police to his door. He broke from his long-standing pattern of targeting strangers and killed someone he knew, Julie Ann Winningham, on March 16, 1995. His signature appeared on a receipt among her possessions. Initially Jesperson denied involvement but then turned himself in after twice attempting suicide. In a subsequent letter to his brother, Brad, he confessed to having committed eight murders over the previous five years.

Jesperson is currently serving three consecutive life sentences in Oregon, and a fourth life sentence was tacked on in California in 2010.

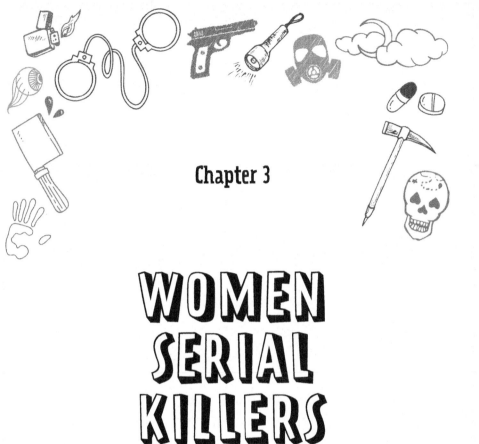

Chapter 3

WOMEN SERIAL KILLERS

Q: What song did serial killer Aileen Wuornos want played at her funeral?

A: Natalie Merchant's "Carnival" was the song of choice for Wuornos, one of the most notorious female serial killers of all time.

Though not the worst in number of victims or gruesome methods, Wuornos is probably the most famous, in large part because of the 2003 film made about her crimes. Charlize Theron won a Best Actress Oscar for portraying Wuornos in the movie *Monster*.

Wuornos' father was a schizophrenic, convicted child rapist who hanged himself without ever meeting his daughter. In 1960, when Wuornos was four years old, her mother abandoned her and her brother. Their grandparents legally adopted them, but by her pre-teens Aileen was already performing sexual favors in exchange for smokes and drugs, possibly even with her own brother. She became pregnant at age 14 after being raped by a cohort of her grandfather. Her child was put up for adoption.

She was also a heavy drinker, and long before the crimes that would make her infamous, Wuornos had a rap sheet full of theft, forgery, firearms possession, robbery, and even assault charges. But it wasn't until she paired up with Tyria Moore—called "Lee" by Wuornos—and began working as a prostitute along Florida's Interstate 75 that she became a murderer.

Over the span of a year Wuornos shot and killed at least seven men, authorities posited, by posing as prostitute with the motive of stealing from them. She had left a bloody palm print on the vehicle of one victim, 65-year-old Peter Seims (whose body was never found), but the real break for authorities came when Wuornos and Moore started pawning items stolen from their victims. Those objects were full of fingerprints, and with Wuornos' prints on file, detectives had an easy time identifying the perpetrator.

In the 1992 trial for the death of her first victim, 51-year-old Richard Mallory, Wuornos famously argued that she had killed him because he had raped her. In fact, this was her claim about all the men's deaths. Something that might have swayed the jury—but which they never heard—was that her first victim had served 10 years for attempted rape in a Maryland psychiatric prison for disturbed offenders. No one had looked for him in the FBI database before the trial, so that information was never brought to light.

In any event, Wuornos was sentenced to death in Florida for the Mallory murder and then pleaded no contest to an additional three, receiving three more death sentences. She maintained her claim that Mallory had violently raped her. Another two death sentences were later tacked on, making six in total.

Wuornos gave up her appeals and fired her attorneys in 2001. "I killed those men, robbed them as cold as ice," she wrote. "And I'd do it again, too." She was executed in 2002 after declining a last meal, requesting only coffee.

Q: What professional wrestler became the Little Old Lady Killer in Mexico City?

A: Juana Barraza was 48 years old when she was arrested for the murder of at least 10 and possibly as many as 40 elderly women. Barraza had been known for portraying "The Lady of Silence" in *lucha libre*, Mexican masked wrestling.

In January 2006, a student staying with an elderly woman in Mexico City came home to find a woman running away from the dead body of her landlady, 82-year-old Ana Maria Reyes, who had been strangled with a stethoscope. The student alerted the police, who chased down Barraza and arrested her. Barraza confessed to killing Reyes but denied responsibility for any other murders. When asked about motive, she said she got "angry." Stories have emerged since then about Barraza's difficult childhood with an alcoholic mother—who for three beers, some say, traded the 12-year-old Barraza to a man who repeatedly raped her and also impregnated her.

The Little Old Lady Killer's method was always the same: she gained entry into the women's homes by pretending to be a social worker or by offering to carry their groceries. She strangled her victims with stockings, scarves, or telephone cords—anything handy, really. Then she stole from them—but only items of insignificant monetary value, such as a religious statue.

Barraza had been able to fool authorities for several years, as they believed the killer was a man disguised as a woman. But then she left a fingerprint at the house of a woman who might have become a victim had her son not arrived home and seen someone fleeing the scene.

That print matched those found at the scenes of five previously unsolved murders, giving police what they needed to link Barraza with the killings and begin building their case.

Q: Actress Veronica Compton had romances with two serial killers. Who were they?

A: Compton had romantic relationships with Kenneth Bianchi, one of the two men responsible for the Hillside Strangler murders, and Douglas Clark. Let's take each relationship in turn, shall we?

Compton was just 24 years old when she was arrested for allegedly trying to strangle a woman to make it look like the Hillside Strangler was still on the loose—which would have benefited Bianchi, who had been arrested for the murders.

Compton and Bianchi had met after the actress and playwright sent Bianchi a copy of her screenplay *The Mutilated Cutter*, about a female serial killer, thinking he would be the perfect beta reader. Compton interviewed Bianchi in jail and fell in love with him over their subsequent discussions of murder fantasies, and Bianchi saw an opportunity. He smuggled her some of his semen in a plastic glove so she could plant it on a victim in a planned copycat Hillside Strangler attack.

Compton never got to the semen part of the plan, though, as the woman she had lured to her room at the Shangri-La Motel in Bellingham, Washington, escaped before Compton could strangle her. Compton was convicted of attempted first-degree murder and sentenced to life in prison. Bianchi continued to correspond with her as she served her time, but Compton's interest was soon sparked by another serial killer, one Douglas Clark.

From death row in California, Clark sent Compton a photo of a head-less female body, and the two corresponded for several years. In 1983 Compton testified at the trial of the other half of the Hillside Strangler duo, Angelo Buono, claiming she agreed to marry Clark to make Bianchi jealous.

Compton was released from prison in 2003.

Q: What was the contribution of Mary Bell, the British Bad Seed, to the UK legal process?

A: Bell was just 11 years old when she was convicted of the manslaughter of Martin Brown, age four, and Brian Howe, age three, in Newcastle in 1968. She had strangled the two little boys on separate occasions.

After serving 12 years, Bell received the good news that at the age of 23 she would be released. But her joy quickly turned to anxiety when the media discovered her identity; she couldn't escape feeling "shaky" in crowds and generally apprehensive in public.

When Bell had a daughter four years later, the court granted her a new identity and "lifelong anonymity" to protect her privacy. Since then, the court has entered similar orders to protect Bell's daughter and grandchild.

Even though Mary Bell doesn't go by that name anymore, it lives on in the UK phrase "Mary Bell order," referring to a court order that protects a convict's identity upon release.

Q: What "Angel of Death" used the catchphrase "This one gets a ticket to God"?

A: Waltraud Wagner was a nurse's aide in a Vienna hospital. Along with Maria Gruber, Irene Leidolf, and Stephanija Mayer, Wagner killed weak but not terminally ill patients in various ways. Their primary method was the "water cure"—holding a patient's nose shut while water was poured down their throat, filling their lungs with fluid and making the death appear "natural." Alternately, these "death angels" injected their victims, both male and female, with large doses of morphine.

Pavilion 5 of the Lainz Hospital was the setting for these atrocious acts between 1983 and 1989. Authorities surmised that the four supposed caregivers targeted patients who complained or annoyed them by doing things such as refusing medication or snoring.

One night a doctor overheard the aides discussing their latest kill, and that led to an investigation and charges against all of them. They initially owned up to 42 deaths but recanted many of those confessions. Some believe they may have killed as many as 200 patients total.

In 1991 Wagner (convicted of 15 murders, 17 attempts, and two counts of aggravated assault) and Leidolf (five murders and two attempts) were each sentenced to life in prison. Mayer received 20 years for attempted murder and manslaughter, and Gruber got 15 for attempted murder.

All have since been released from prison.

Q: Can you name the niece of the king of Poland who was arguably the worst female serial killer in history?

A: Erzsebet (Elizabeth) Báthory, a member of a well-established noble Hungarian family, may have tortured and killed upwards of 650 young girls some four centuries ago.

Báthory was betrothed at a young age to Count Ferenc Nádasdy but kept her own surname because her family outranked his. Upon their union, dear Erzsebet made sure that all her homes were equipped with torture chambers and dungeons, where she delighted in such activities as piercing the nipples of her victims—her own servants and, later, people procured by scouring the local countryside with the help of employees.

Báthory also drank her victims' blood, believing it would keep her young. She stabbed, burnt, bit, and beat some victims, while she starved others to death. As tools of her torture trade she was particularly fond of scissors, branding irons, whips, red-hot irons, coins, keys, and pins and needles.

She. Was. Awful.

One night in 1610, she got busted in the act during a raid by her neighbor, Count Gyorgy Thurzo, who had been authorized to do so by the reigning King Matthias II. Several in-house accomplices were arrested with her—and surprise, surprise, only they were tried, convicted, and executed (one got life in prison).

Báthory, on the other hand, didn't even face a trial. Instead she was placed under house arrest in her castle, in a bricked-up room with just slits for ventilation and food tray delivery. She lived out the rest of her life there—all four years or so of it.

Q: Who was the first known "black widow" in the United States?

A: Belle Gunness arrived in Chicago from Norway in 1881 as Brynhild Paulsdatter Storset. She adopted an American name and became infamous for killing off loved ones to collect insurance proceeds, even placing "lonely hearts" ads to find victims—er, suitors. She is alternately known as "Lady Bluebeard."

In 1884 she married a fellow Norwegian immigrant, Mads Sorenson, and for the first 12 years of their marriage things seemed to be going fine. Then came the 1886 fire at their confectioner's shop, sparked by a kerosene lamp that was never found. The couple purchased a home with the insurance money, but two years later that, too, burned to the ground—though again, at least they had insurance.

In the meantime, two of the couple's children died of "acute colitis," which with a modern eye could have been poisoning. Then, in 1900, husband Mads died after Belle had given him a "powder" to cure his cold. No autopsy was performed. And yes, all of their lives had been insured and Belle collected the money.

The widow left Chicago for La Porte, Indiana, with three children in tow—two of her own plus her niece. In 1902 she married another Norwegian, Peter Gunness, who died just eight months later when a meat grinder fell on his head and cracked his skull. During this time Belle delivered a son and her niece disappeared, with the explanation that she had gone west to a finishing school.

Twice widowed but with a farm to keep, Belle began placing ads in local newspapers, one of which read as follows:

"Rich. Good-looking widow. Young. Owner of a large farm. Wishes to get in touch with a gentleman of wealth and cultured tastes. Object: matrimony. Triflers need not apply."

Non-triflers began appearing—though never leaving.

In 1908 the farm burned down, and in the charred remains were the bodies of three children along with the headless corpse of a woman, with no skull to be found. Authorities assumed Belle had died in the fire, and her handyman, Randy Lamphere, was arrested for arson and murder. Later he was convicted of just arson.

Then more bodies turned up in subsequent searches of the property. How many men Belle killed is a point of controversy, but it is thought the number could be as high as 30. One of the corpses was positively identified as Belle's niece, a few others as potential suitors who had answered Belle's ads.

What about Belle herself, though? Lamphere insisted that the headless corpse belonged to a woman who was picked up at a saloon and brought home to be murdered as a stand-in for Belle. He claimed that he had driven Belle to the railway station for her getaway. She was supposed to get in touch when she was in the clear, he said.

She never did, though, said Lamphere, and despite many alleged Belle "sightings" in Indiana, Ohio, Iowa, and even California over the next few decades, she was never located again.

Lamphere allegedly told a different story in a confession to a reverend. He said he had gone to the farm with a woman on the night of the fire to steal the money he believed was owed to him after years of helping Belle dispose of bodies. He claimed he had used the same chloroform Belle used on her suitors—whose heads she would chop off with an axe if the chloroform didn't work—to kill Belle and the children, including the niece. He said the fire must have started when a candle they had been using tipped over.

That story, of course, doesn't explain the headless corpse. And Belle's mystery lives on.

Q: Who was the female half of the Moors Murders duo?

A: Myra Hindley, with partner Ian Brady, killed and buried five children on the Saddleworth Moor in England's greater Manchester area in the mid-1960s, though one body has never been found. When news of their horrendous crimes spread, the couple became the most hated people in the UK—but a different angle later emerged.

From jail and then through her private papers, which she turned over to authorities just before she died in 2002, Hindley alleged—sometimes in graphic detail—that Brady had drugged, raped, and assaulted her regularly and threatened harm to her family if she didn't take part in his abhorrent acts.

Their young victims included two 12-year-old boys, John Kilbride and Keith Bennett; 16-year-old Pauline Reade; 17-year-old Edward Evans; and 10-year-old Lesley Ann Downey, whose screams echoed through the courtroom during the murder trial. Brady had recorded her murder on a 16-minute-long audiotape that was played for the jury. At least four of the victims were sexually assaulted before their deaths.

Brady and Hindley were apprehended after Hindley's brother-in-law, David Smith, witnessed Brady killing Evans. When Smith told Maureen, his wife and Hindley's sister, she insisted they tell the authorities. The subsequent search for evidence turned up a suitcase of Brady's that had been left at the Manchester Central railway station. Inside were photos of a naked little girl, a scarf in her mouth, shown in pornographic poses. The girl was Downey. After finding additional photos clearly taken on the moors, the police searched and came across an arm bone poking through the ground, which turned out to be Downey's.

Hindley's sentence of life imprisonment without the possibility of parole marked the first time in modern history that a woman had faced such a penalty in the UK. Hindley tried to get early release several times before her death, but Brady—who was declared legally insane in 1985—readily admitted he shouldn't be in society. He died at Ashworth Hospital in 2017.

Q: What was the real name of Sexy Sadie, convicted of murder as part of the Manson Family?

A: Susan Atkins believed that Charles Manson was Jesus, and she became part of his "family" at their Southern California ranch in the late 1960s. As one of his followers she was known as Sadie Mae Glutz, and she would forever be identified with the group that busted into the home of film director Roman Polanski and actress Sharon Tate on August 8, 1969, and killed the pregnant Tate and four others. Initially Atkins said she had held down Tate while Charles "Tex" Watson stabbed her, but she later said she simply watched.

Before the Tate murder, Atkins was one of four people who had gone to the home of a man named Gary Hinman to try to get money from him. Hinman wasn't cooperative. Manson slashed the man's face and left, leaving the other three to kill Hinman.

Later, while being held for that murder, Atkins started speaking with Virginia Graham, a fellow detainee at the Sybil Brand Institute, about the Tate murder. Atkins said the group had wanted to commit a crime that would "shock the world."

According to Graham she told Tate, "Look, bitch, I don't care about you. I don't care if you're going to have a baby. You had better be ready. You're going to die, and I don't feel anything about it."

Then she killed Tate, and she explained how that felt. "I felt so elated; tired, but at peace with myself. I knew this was just the beginning of helter skelter. Now the world would listen."

"Helter Skelter" was Manson's plan for an apocalyptic race war.

The day after those murders, the "family"—including Atkins—killed grocer Leno Labianca and his wife Rosemary in their home.

The circus-like atmosphere of the ensuing trial only added to the Manson mystique. In one newspaper photo, a broadly smiling Atkins is holding hands with fellow Manson family members Patricia Krenwinkel and Leslie Van Houten. "Charlie's Girls" sang and chanted while court was in session, getting them booted from proceedings at one point.

Atkins, who said she was a born-again Christian who had found God in prison, was sentenced to death in 1971. Her sentence was commuted to life imprisonment when California abolished the death penalty by statute in 1972. (The death penalty was later reinstated by a referendum vote, but previous capital sentences were not reinstated.) While living at Manson's ranch, Atkins had given birth to a son, Zezozose Zadfrack Glutz, but her parental rights were terminated upon her conviction, and the boy was placed with an adoptive family.

"Sexy Sadie" died of natural causes at the Central California Women's facility in Chowchilla in 2009; at that time she was the longest-serving prisoner in California. Her husband, James Whitehouse, who often represented her at her unsuccessful parole hearings, claims her last word was "Amen."

Q: What Italian serial killer made soap with her victims' body parts?

A: Leonarda Cianciulli is called *La Saponificatrice* or the Soap Maker of Correggio because she was convicted of bludgeoning three women to death in 1939 and 1940 and then making soap with their body parts. She boiled the fat from the bodies and then shared her homemade creations, which also included cakes, with her neighbors.

Cianciulli's beloved son, Giuseppe, was the one suspected of committing the murders, but the devoted mother confessed to the crimes and gave details.

If you are thinking that this sounds like an Italian mother who may have been protecting her son, you're not alone. Recently two Italian authors have cast doubt on the tales Cianciulli recounted in her 800-page prison diary, especially concerning the likelihood that she made soap and cakes with human remains. Fabio Sanvitale and Vincenzo Mastronardi assert that Leonarda was not mentally ill at all (though she lived out her final days in an asylum) but instead was a cold, clever, calculating woman who told lie after lie and made herself into a myth.

And there's no doubt that Cianciulli was into legends and superstitions. Her belief that the only way to keep Giuseppe safe as he entered the Italian Army was through human sacrifice apparently sparked her killing and soap-making.

Beyond that, she also believed her mother had cursed her after Cianciulli married someone other than the man her parents had chosen. In fact, over the course of her life she was imprisoned for fraud, had her home destroyed by an earthquake, and lost 13 of 17 children either through miscarriage or early death. A fortune teller's prediction that she had prison and a criminal asylum in her future only deepened the woman's belief that her life would always be bleak.

Cianciulli died in an asylum in Pozzuoli, outside of Naples, in 1970 at the age 76.

Q: What diagnosis did psychiatrists offer for Marybeth Tinning after she lost nine children?

A: Munchausen's syndrome by proxy was the diagnosis when nine Tinning children died between 1972 and 1985. This is a condition in which someone responsible for caring for another intentionally harms them or exaggerates their symptoms to gain attention or sympathy for themselves.

In 1987 Tinning was convicted of the 1985 murder of her ninth child, four-month-old Tami Lynne, after an autopsy revealed the infant had died from asphyxia by suffocation. The Schenectady, New York, mother was also indicted in the deaths of two of her sons and even admitted to smothering them along with Tami Lynne—she said it was because she was "not a good mother"—but she was only prosecuted for the one death. She was sentenced to 20 years to life in prison.

Tinning's first child died in 1972, and authorities believe that death wasn't suspicious. Eight-day-old Jennifer had never left the hospital, and an autopsy showed she had died of acute meningitis.

Two-year-old son Joseph Jr. died just three weeks later. No autopsy was performed; the cause of death was believed to be a viral infection and a seizure disorder. Four-year-old Barbara died six weeks after that—of "cardiac arrest," as doctors couldn't find another cause.

The other children's deaths were said to be the result of pulmonary edema, sudden infant death syndrome (SIDS), and bronchial pneumonia. One child's cause of death wasn't ever determined.

The theory was that Tinning enjoyed the attention that came with the tragic death of her first child, so she pursued that feeling again and again with the rest of her children.

She was granted parole in 2018 at the age of 75.

Q: Who was the female half of the couple who targeted fellow black people across the Midwest?

A: Debra Denise Brown got mixed up with convicted rapist Alton Coleman in 1983, and the pair embarked on a killing binge in May of 1984. Their relationship has been labeled "master-slave," as Brown had a low IQ and a dependent personality and had never been violent before meeting Coleman. At the time the two went on the road, Coleman was already scheduled to face sexual assault charges concerning a 14-year-old girl.

The couple targeted black neighborhoods so as not to arouse suspicion and preyed on both children and the elderly. Their first victims were nine-year-old Vernita Wheat and her mother Juanita in Kenosha, Wisconsin. Three weeks later, they tied up and sexually assaulted two young girls, ages seven and nine, in Gary, Indiana; the older girl survived, but Tamika Turks did not. The next to die was 25-year-old Donna Williams, also of Gary, though her body wasn't found until nearly a month later, in Detroit. She had been raped and strangled.

A few weeks later, the couple was in Dearborn Heights, Michigan, where they broke into the home of a couple to beat and rob them. From there Coleman and Brown moved on to Toledo, Ohio, where they wound up at the home of Virginia Temple. Relatives found Temple and her nine-year-old daughter Rachelle dead, both strangled. Still in Toledo, the duo invaded another home, tied up and robbed the couple inside, but left them alive.

Coleman and Brown moved on to Cincinnati, and on July 12 they raped and strangled 15-year-old Tonnie Storey. On that day Coleman was placed on the FBI's Ten Most Wanted List as an addendum, but the couple simply moved on to Norwood, Ohio. There they brutally beat Harry and Marlene Waters to death, also raping Marlene. They stole the dead couple's car and kidnapped a college professor, locking him in the trunk. He was later found alive.

In their last hurrah, Coleman and Brown stole the car of a reverend and his wife and set off for Illinois once again—though on their way, they stopped to carjack and murder 75-year-old Eugene Scott in Indianapolis.

The pair was arrested in Evanston, and Coleman ended up with death sentences in three states: Ohio, Indiana, and Illinois. In 2002 he was executed by lethal injection in Ohio while 18 witnesses from six different victim families watched. A psychiatrist who had interviewed Coleman described him as incapable of emotion.

Brown's Ohio death sentence was commuted to life in prison. In early 2019 the Indiana Attorney General's office announced it would also withdraw its demand for capital punishment for Brown, based on her intellectual disability.

Q: What baby-killing nurse is facing new charges dating back to the early 1980s?

A: In 1985 Genene Jones was convicted of injecting a fatal dose of the muscle relaxant succinylcholine into 15-month-old Chelsea McClellan at the Kerr County Clinic in Texas and was sentenced to 99 years in prison. She was also convicted of attempting to administer an overdose of the blood thinner heparin to one-month-old Rolando Santos and was sentenced to 60 years in that case, with the sentences to run concurrently.

But then Texas passed a law to relieve prison crowding, and Jones could have gotten out in 2018. That's when Bexar County District Attorney Nicholas "Nico" LaHood stepped in with a big ole "nope." He got Jones indicted for five infant murders committed in 1981 and 1982, and bail set at $1 million on each charge has meant that Jones remains in prison awaiting trial.

This "angel of death" had long been suspected of being responsible for baby deaths at Bexar County's Medical Center Hospital in San Antonio; fellow nurses referred to Jones' work hours as "the death shift."

While in prison, Jones reportedly admitted "killing those babies" to two separate parole officials, referring to murders for which she had not been convicted. According to a fellow inmate, Jones said that "voices" in her head had killed the babies. Because of Jones' public, often exaggerated attempts to save the infants who died in her care, as well as expressions of grief upon their demise, some mental health professionals believe she has histrionic disorder and/or Munchausen's syndrome by proxy.

In February 2019, the judge in Jones' case announced that a psychologist has declared Jones competent to stand trial.

Q: What "jolly" nurse killed 31 people around the turn of the 20th century?

A: Jane Toppan trained at Cambridge Hospital in Massachusetts but left short of a diploma when two of her patients died mysteriously. That didn't stop her from working as a nurse, though; she simply forged a certificate and got work privately. She was apparently quite affable, earning her the nickname Jolly Jane.

Toppan enjoyed seeing how her patients' nervous systems reacted to different combinations and doses of drugs, so she administered opioids, morphine, and atropine at will. After she was caught, she said she had derived sexual pleasure from bringing her patients to the brink of death and then either reviving them by adjusting the medication— or killing them. She invariably lay in bed and held her patients as they died, but whether she had sex with them before or after their deaths is unknown.

In 1899 she poisoned her foster sister Elizabeth with strychnine. Toppan also murdered the family's housekeeper and a sister of her brother-in-law and tried to kill her brother-in-law as well, but he recovered.

In 1901 the entire family of Alden Davis died within the span of about a month. First was Davis' wife Mattie who had been visiting Toppan to collect rent from the jolly nurse when she died. When one of the Davis' married daughters, Geraldine Gordon, went to retrieve the body, Toppan traveled with her back to Cape Cod—and Gordon quickly fell ill and died as well. Davis himself got sick during a business trip to Boston and was nursed to death by Toppan upon his return. The final family member, the other married daughter, Minnie Gibbs, died shortly thereafter. Autopsies of the bodies of Gordon and Gibbs revealed large quantities of arsenic.

Toppan was arrested in October 1901 and initially confessed to 31 murders (though authorities only definitively linked her to 11), but later she said the total could have been as high as 100. She attempted suicide several times throughout her life. Toppan was found not guilty by reason of "inherited insanity" for her crimes; both her father and sister had spent time in mental institutions. She died in an asylum in 1938.

Q: How did Vera Renczi, a "female Bluebeard" from Romania, murder 35 men?

A: Renczi sprinkled arsenic in their wine and food, sometimes even creating a ceremonial "last supper." Her victims included two husbands, a son, and 32 lovers.

An ethnic Hungarian woman born in Bucharest, Romania, Renczi was called a "female Bluebeard" in newspaper accounts at the time. Her killings occurred at her home in Berkerekul, Yugoslavia, now Serbia.

She was caught in 1925 after a young woman notified police that her husband, banker Leo Pachich, had gone missing after going to visit Renczi. Upon pushing past a stubborn housekeeper who had to be handcuffed so they could get by, officers found 35 coffins in the basement. Each was labeled with the name and age of the deceased.

The killings began with Renczi's first husband, with whom she had a son. He went away on what was said to be a year-long business trip; the conniving woman began mourning after two years. Another husband lasted only four months before his, ahem, "long trip" began. After that, the "rich and distinguished widow" (as the neighbors saw her) became a source of gossip known as the Mysterious Huntress because she frequented town cafés nightly in search of young men.

Her method was to stare at her chosen man—usually a non-local—until he felt compelled to follow her. Then, with a rather unoriginal pickup line, she'd ask if he wanted to see her house. The men would stay with her a week, maybe more, and then the huntress would be back out on the prowl.

Her motive? "They were men," Renczi insisted. "I could not endure the thought that they would ever put their arms around another woman after they had embraced me."

She said her son had "threatened to betray" her. "He was a man, too," she said. "Soon he would have held another woman in his arms." Some accounts say he discovered the coffins and threatened to turn her in.

Renczi's extreme jealousy dated to her childhood, when she overheard her father saying he was going to give her beloved dog away. She poisoned it so no one else could have it. "When he leaves me he leaves this world," the young Renczi said.

She was sentenced to life in prison after being convicted of 35 murders and died there.

Caveat: Some believe this entire story is a hoax, because the only sources for it are American newspaper accounts from 1925 and no supporting documentation has been found in Serbia.

Q: Who was the youngest woman ever sentenced to death in the US?

A: Judith Neelley was just 18 years old—and a mother of three—in 1983 when she was sentenced to die in the electric chair for the kidnapping, rape, and murder of 13-year-old Lisa Millican. In 1999, just three days before her scheduled execution, Alabama Governor Fob James commuted her sentence to life in prison with the possibility of parole.

She came up for parole for the first time in May 2018 but was denied. Neelley told the parole board that she didn't feel she should be released yet and noted that "God has changed my heart and life" greatly during her 36 years in prison.

"In order to spare the Millican family the pain and trauma of having to attend the hearing," she wrote in a letter to the board, "I have agreed to waive my right to be considered for parole at this time."

Neelley admits to killing Millican with her partner-in-crime, husband Alvin, after taking her from outside a mall in Rome, Georgia in September of 1982. The girl had been on an outing with other residents of the Ethel Harpst Home for children in Cedartown. The couple transported the girl to a Scottsboro, Alabama motel, where they both raped her repeatedly over three days. Then they took her to the Little River Canyon in Fort Payne, and Judith injected Millican several times with drain cleaner. When that didn't kill her, she shot the still-conscious girl in the back and dumped her body in the canyon.

Back in Rome the following week, Judith approached a young couple, Janice Chatman and John Hancock, and asked them if they wanted to go to a party. The two agreed but were instead taken to a secluded area and shot. Hancock survived and identified Judith as the one with the gun.

Just a couple of weeks later, the pair was arrested for writing bad checks, and an eyewitness to the Chatman and Hancock abduction recognized Judith and her children. Alvin insisted the crimes were Judith's idea and claimed his wife had killed at least 15 people. Despite police efforts, no other murders have been linked to them.

At trial, Judith claimed Alvin had abused her daily, including beatings with a baseball bat and a pistol, and that she committed crimes "because Al told me to" in order to procure sex partners for him. Joann Browning, Alvin's first wife, testified at Judith's trial that she, too, would have killed to escape Al's wrath.

Judith had run away with the married-with-children, 25-year-old Alvin and was pregnant with twins by age 16. She delivered the babies while in custody at a Macon Youth Development Campus after the couple had robbed an elderly woman at gunpoint. Judith delivered her third child while in jail awaiting trial for Millican's murder.

Alvin pleaded guilty to murder in Georgia and was sentenced to life in prison. Alabama authorities couldn't definitively link him to the vile acts in that state, so he wasn't tried for Millican's death.

Q: Who was the "death angel" who reportedly stabbed herself in her vagina with scissors?

A: Bobbie Sue Terrell had a long history of self-injury and mental illness before she was charged in the 1984 deaths of four patients who had been under her care at the North Horizon Health Care Center in St. Petersburg, Florida. She is said to have stabbed herself in the vagina because she was frustrated with her inability to bear children.

A registered nurse, Terrell was married to Daniel Dudley when she learned she wouldn't be able to have children naturally. When their adopted son was hospitalized for a drug overdose, Dudley accused her of giving the boy her own schizophrenia medicine.

Terrell worked in Illinois for a while but lost her job after exhibiting odd behavior, including the vaginal stabbing incident. In November 1984 she moved to Florida and became a night supervisor at North Horizon, often the only RN on duty overnight. And the deaths began—12 in less than two weeks.

Then Terrell claimed an intruder had stabbed her, but the strong suspicion was that she had done it to herself. Psychiatric evaluations throughout her life—she had checked herself into mental institutions at least twice—labeled Terrell as borderline schizophrenic with Munchausen's syndrome by proxy, which causes individuals to create or exaggerate medical issues for sympathy.

As she faced suspension of her Florida nursing license (she was already under investigation in Illinois regarding her license there) Terrell (then

"Dudley") married Ron Terrell and took his last name. Not long after that she was involuntarily committed for psychiatric treatment.

By then investigators were hot on the trail of this "angel of death," having exhumed bodies in Florida, Pennsylvania, Texas, and Wisconsin. Terrell was charged with first-degree murder for asphyxiating Aggie Marsh (age 97), injecting something into Leathy McKnight (85) and Mary Carter (79), and both asphyxiating and injecting Stella Bradham (85). She also faced an attempted murder charge for injecting another patient with insulin.

Terrell pled guilty to second-degree murder and was sentenced to 60 years' imprisonment. She died in prison in 2007.

Q: Why did Dorothea Puente murder tenants in her Sacramento boardinghouse?

A: Puente's motive for killing her seven victims in the 1980s was cold hard cash in the form of their Social Security checks. Her method was to poison them with prescription drugs. Authorities say Puente managed to collect more than $5,000 a month for years with this scheme.

From the outside, the light blue Victorian on F Street in California's capital city was a beautiful, distinguished home that provided a temporary stay for those who needed help; she took in—elderly, mentally ill, homeless, and substance-abusing boarders. But what lurked in its backyard stunned the neighborhood—and the world—in 1988 when police started digging. Tipped off by a tenant who noted the large holes that had been filled behind the house, investigators looking into the disappearance of a social worker's client uncovered a decomposing human foot and a leg bone. And that was just the beginning.

Puente buried four women and three men, ages 52 to 79, even removing the head, hands, and feet of one victim to hinder identification. She gave her tenants lethal mixtures of prescription drugs, such as codeine, acetaminophen, and a variety of antidepressants and tranquilizers. All of the dead had the sedative Dalmane in their systems; Puente had a steady prescription for the drug between 1985 and 1988.

It is difficult to imagine a more innocuous-looking landlady than the 1980s version of Puente: 5'2" tall, white-haired, with a garden of well-tended roses. She was known for being extremely supportive of the local Hispanic community and even counseled women going through difficult divorces. On the other hand, she faked cancer for many years and was reportedly an alcoholic who threw adult temper tantrums featuring flying furniture and obscenities.

In 1993 Puente faced nine murder charges; investigators also believed her responsible for two additional deaths. She was only convicted on three counts after jurors deliberated for 24 days—the longest deliberation time for a murder case in California history.

Puente died in 2011 at the Central California Women's Facility in Chowchilla. She was 82.

Her house, however, lives on. In September 2018, the current owners hosted an exhibit called "Art to Die For." They readily admit to trying to have fun with curiosity seekers by posting signs such as "Trespassers will be drugged and buried in the yard."

Q: What offhand threat by Rosemary and Fred West to their children led authorities to nine bodies?

A: The British couple told their children that if they didn't behave, they would "end up under the patio like Heather." That comment, relayed to childcare workers, along with Fred West's arrest for raping his 13-year-old daughter in 1992 and Rosemary's (Rose's) arrest for child cruelty, led investigators to look more closely at the pair.

Heather, the couple's oldest child, had disappeared in 1987. Her parents claimed she had run off to Wales with a lesbian partner. They never so much as filed a missing persons report, and it became clear why in 1994 when police showed up to excavate the couple's garden. The search revealed Heather's body along with a third human thigh bone, so they kept digging.

Heather was far from the Wests' first victim, but no one could have imagined the extent of their depravity in what the British press called the House of Horrors. The couple abducted at least six girls or young women from local bus stops, then sexually abused and tortured them for days before killing, dismembering, and burying them.

Fred had also killed his children's nanny, 18-year-old Anna McFall, while he was still married to his first wife, Rena. Anna had been pregnant with Fred's child at the time. In 1971 Rose killed Rena's eight-year-old daughter, Charmaine, and when Fred returned from a prison stint for theft a couple weeks later, he dismembered the young girl's body and buried it. Then he killed Rena when she came looking for Charmaine. In 1977 Shirley Robinson, another woman pregnant with a child of Fred's, wound up dead.

The couple was arrested in 1994, and Rose immediately began the campaign to save herself. Distancing herself from her husband and the crimes, she said she hadn't been a willing participant and had even tried to stop them. Fred hanged himself in his prison cell on New Year's Day in 1995.

Rose was convicted of 10 murders and given life imprisonment without the possibility of parole; she was only the second woman in Britain to receive this sentence, Myra Hindley being the first.

Rose is still in prison and has given up all her appeals. Their house at 25 Cromwell Street in Gloucester was torn down in 1996 after excavations left it unstable, and all that remains at that location is a footpath that links Cromwell Street with Brunswick Square.

Q: Who was the first woman executed in Ohio's electric chair?

A: Serial killer Anna Marie Hahn met her death in the electric chair in 1938 after being convicted of poisoning four men. Although many reports portray her as a caretaker to these men, the confession penned by Hahn in prison and published in the *Cincinnati Enquirer* after she was electrocuted suggests she was heavily in debt—she expressed a particular fondness for the racetrack—and took extreme measures to get out of it.

Hahn was a native of Germany but landed in Cincinnati after she had an illegitimate child in Germany. Little Oscar was left behind in Bavaria, but only until Hahn met her husband-to-be Philip, whose surname she assumed when they married.

Hahn was convicted of killing Jacob Wagner, though in her confession she admits to killing three others as well—George Gsellman, George Obendorfer, and Albert Palmer. About this last gentleman she has the most to say, claiming that she owed him money and he was pressuring her to "be his girl." One night when he came over with oysters, she casually sprinkled some rat poison on them; Palmer died shortly thereafter.

It's questionable whether Hahn's confession is true, as she was compensated for it and the money went to her son. He received a new name and family after his mother's death.

For her last meal, Hahn ordered fried chicken, which the prison warden prepared, but the doomed woman couldn't bear to eat it. She couldn't manage to get dressed, either; she faced death wearing her pajamas, her stockings pooled around her ankles.

Q: Who is the "black widow" who got away with murdering most of her family in France?

A: Marie Besnard almost certainly administered arsenic to various loved ones over the course of 20 years in Loudun, France. Expert witnesses failed to effectively deliver scientific evidence at her trials, however, and she was acquitted—three times.

Besnard grew up modestly, and her plan for acquiring wealth involved killing off members of her family and another unlucky couple, and burying their bodies in what the locals came to call "Arsenic Corner"— the section of the town graveyard that held her victims. Caught up in Besnard's greedy web of poison were her parents, her great aunt, two husbands, the parents and sister of her second husband, two cousins, and a couple who happened to have a house she fancied.

Police went digging after neighbor Louise Pintou (with whom Besnard's husband Leon may have been having an affair) who told them that Leon, from his deathbed, said he saw his wife put something in his bowl before the soup went in. Not long after, everything that Leon had given to Pintou was stolen from her house. Leon's widow blamed his death on rancid fat she had used to prepare dinner, but authorities headed straight to Arsenic Corner and found that 11 of the 12 bodies there contained lethal levels of arsenic.

Besnard's scheme had been working out well for her up to that point. By 1947 she had accumulated $30,000, two farms, 120 acres, and three inns. She was even able to hire a strapping young German POW farmhand named Alfred Dietz, which got the locals talking.

Alas, prosecutors never got murder charges to stick. Scientific testimony was still touch and go at that point, and the medical professionals called to the stand didn't convince the jurors. In one trial, Dr. Pierre Beroud boasted that he could pick out arsenic on sight. Besnard's clever lawyer, Albert Gautrat—apparently the "if it doesn't fit, you must acquit" Johnnie Cochran of his day—quickly put Beroud to the test with six test tubes and asked the good doctor to identify which contained arsenic.

"Numbers two and three," Beroud proclaimed.

Nope. The right answer was none of them.

Besnard did spend five years in detention during the course of her trials, but she lived out the rest of her life as a free woman. She died of natural causes in 1980 at the age of 82 and donated her body to … science, of course.

Q: Who is the Giggling Granny who poisoned four husbands across four states?

A: In 1955, to avoid the death penalty, Nannie Doss pleaded guilty to murdering her fifth husband, Samuel Doss, in Oklahoma by putting rat poison in his prunes and coffee. The portly woman smacked on gum, smiled, and laughed throughout the proceedings, giving her the nickname Giggling Granny.

Regarding Samuel, the murderess told police, "He wouldn't buy me a radio or television set and was mean to me."

Doss also admitted to poisoning three other husbands, each of whom she had met through lonely hearts ads. She always believed in "good, clean romance," she said. Samuel was reportedly a church-going man who didn't approve of his wife's love of romance novels.

The first to die was actually her second husband, Frank Harrelson, who drank rat poison–laced corn whiskey in Alabama. Next was Harley (or Arlie) Lanning in North Carolina, and the third was Richard L. Morton in Kansas. Her first husband, Charles Braggs, escaped Doss' wrath when he left with one of their two daughters, afraid his wife might have poisoned their two recently deceased daughters. Braggs said her food didn't "taste right."

Doss denied accusations of other possible poisonings, such as those of her grandson and mother—whose death was, indeed, from arsenic. Still, several other people around her over the years had died suddenly, including her sister Dovie, a mother-in-law, and her daughter's newborn, so there's no telling how many people met their fates at the hand of Doss.

One of the psychiatrists at her sanity trial labeled Doss as "infantile and retarded," and the psychiatric report from Oklahoma's Eastern State Hospital said she was "mentally defective." As a child Doss had suffered a terrible head injury in a train accident, which she said made her wonder whether she "might be thinking crooked."

In any event, the judge thought it would set a "poor precedent" for Doss to be the first woman sentenced to death in Oklahoma, so he spared her life. Doss worked in the prison bakery (what?) before she died of leukemia in 1965.

Q: Who was just the third British woman sentenced to life imprisonment with no possibility of parole?

A: Joanna Dennehy was given the UK's harshest sentence in 2014 for the murders of three men in eastern England in 2013. In the span of 10 days, the 31-year-old Dennehy ruthlessly stabbed the men—all of whom she knew—through the heart and then went in search of strangers to attack in western England.

Her first victim was Lukasz Slaboszewski, age 31, who apparently thought Dennehy was his girlfriend. The second was Dennehy's housemate, 56-year-old John Chapman, and the third was her land-lord and boss, Kevin Lee, age 48. All three bodies were dumped into ditches near Peterborough, but Dennehy went out of her way to humiliate Lee by posing his corpse with his backside exposed from under a black sequined dress.

After those murders, an accomplice named Gary Stretch helped her locate additional victims in Hereford. There Dennehy stabbed two men out walking their dogs, about nine minutes apart. She even stole the second guy's dog.

Dennehy had been under psychiatric care in 2012, diagnosed with being psychopathic as well as having personality, emotional, and anti-social disorders. She was also on probation for assault and for harboring a dangerous dog. A probation report found that she had the "potential to cause serious harm," but that she probably wouldn't do so.

Dennehy, who said she killed "to see if I was as cold as I thought I was," smiled as her sentence was read. The only other UK women to receive life imprisonment with no chance for parole are Myra Hindley (1966) and Rosemary West (1995).

Q: Shirley Winters is unique among female serial killers for one type of crime. What was it?

A: Arson is what makes Winters unique. Dating back to 1979, Winters has been connected with at least 17 fires, either at homes she lived in or at homes that were owned by loved ones in upstate New York. In 1997 she was convicted of setting fire to her late mother's house, and she served eight years for that crime.

Her serial killing, though, encompassed far more than fire. A shocking trail of crimes began to unravel in 2006 when 23-month-old Ryan Rivers died in his grandparents' bathtub while Winters was staying with the family. Police quickly linked her to the drowning, and that caused authorities to look further into the deaths of her own three children: infant Ronald (who supposedly died of sudden infant death syndrome in 1980) and three-year-old Colleen and 20-month-old John (both of whom perished in a house fire in 1979).

Authorities determined that Ronald had been smothered and that the other two children had suffered head injuries before the fire began.

In 2008 Winters agreed to plead guilty to first-degree manslaughter in the deaths of her son Ronald and the Rivers child, and prosecutors agreed not to pursue charges against her in the deaths of her other two children. Winters received sentences of eight to 25 years for her son's death and 20 years for Rivers' death, to be served concurrently—making her eligible for parole in 2025.

"She's been good at only two things in her life—setting fires and killing children," said Onondaga County District Attorney William Fitzpatrick of Winters after sentencing.

Harsh, for sure, but Fitzpatrick defended his comments. He said he was directing them toward whomever would be considering Winters' parole requests in the future, hoping they will "if at all possible keep her locked up for as long as the law allows."

Q: Who was the female half of the Love Slave Killers?

A: Charlene and Gerald Gallego raped, tortured, and killed 10 people across California, Oregon, and Nevada between 1978 and 1980.

As a child, Charlene's tested at the genius IQ level, and she possessed incredible talent for the violin, but unfortunately she fell into drug and alcohol abuse. She had already been married twice when she met Gerald at age 21.

Gerald was 10 years her senior and had been married five times previously. His trouble with the law began at age seven. As an adult, he had arrests, convictions, and outstanding warrants piled up on several charges, including rape and incest relating to his daughter, Mary Ellen. Gerald's estranged father was the first man to be executed in Mississippi's gas chamber.

In search of the perfect sex slave for her man, Charlene helped him kidnap, rape, and murder six teenage girls, a pregnant 21-year-old woman who was buried alive on a beach, a 34-year-old woman, and a couple in their early 20s.

The Gallegos' last victims were college sweethearts Craig Miller and Mary Beth Sowers in Sacramento, California. Miller's fraternity brother had seen the abduction and took down the license plate number; police traced the car to Charlene's parents. After Charlene called her parents asking for money, the FBI was waiting at the Western Union office in Omaha, Nebraska.

Eventually Charlene flipped on Gerald in exchange for a reduced prison sentence of 16 years and eight months. Representing himself at trial,

Gallego argued that he had diminished capacity thanks to a quart and a half of tequila and various drugs, and also that Charlene had killed Sowers. He was convicted of the murders of both college students and sentenced to death, then received another death sentence in Nevada for two other murders.

The Pershing County District Attorney Richard Wagner, who prosecuted Gerald in California, called him "a domineering sexual psychopath" and said Charlene's "whole life was spent trying to please him."

Charlene was released in 1997, while Gerald died of cancer in prison in 2002.

Chapter 4

INTERNATIONAL SERIAL KILLERS

Q: How did Abul Djabar of Afghanistan kill his victims?

A: Djabar used his turban to strangle at least 65 young men and boys and possibly more than 300 from the 1960s into 1970 in Afghanistan's Kabul Province—hence his "Turban Killer" nickname.

Djabar killed his victims while raping them and was caught in the act in October 1970. By that time, two innocent men had been hanged for his crimes.

The loved ones of Djabar's victims didn't have to wait long for justice once he was arrested, though. Quite possibly the worst serial killer in Afghanistan history was tried and publicly hanged within days.

Q: Daniel Camargo Barbosa, who murdered scores of young girls and women, is also noted for something else. What is it?

A: *El sádico del Charquito* (The Sadist of Charquito) was notorious not only for his brutal treatment of victims in Colombia and Ecuador during the 1970s and 1980s but also because he managed to escape from Gorgona prison—aka the Colombian Alcatraz—through the shark-infested waters surrounding it.

Camargo reportedly became obsessed with raping young girls and women as part of a pact formed with his lover, Esperanza. He planned to marry Esperanza, but since she was not a virgin they concocted a plan to find him virgins. The two worked together to lure young girls to their apartment, where the girls were drugged and raped. In 1964 Camargo was convicted of the sexual assault of an eight-year-old girl in Colombia.

In 1974, a couple years after his release, Camargo abducted a nine-year-old girl and raped her. This time he murdered his victim so she couldn't report the crime, but he was tracked down and arrested anyway. Authorities believed that Camargo's body count could have been as high as 80, though he was convicted of raping and murdering just the nine-year-old.

Camargo was sentenced to 25 years on Gorgona.

In 1984 he escaped the island prison by fashioning a makeshift boat and navigating the ocean currents he had studied intensively. Many believed he had died on the journey, but Camargo resurfaced in

Ecuador and started a new bout of raping and killing that lasted two years.

In March 1986, Ecuadorian police announced that they had captured a "psychopathic-paranoiac-sado-masochist" suspected in the deaths of 47 young girls and women, ranging in age from nine to 28. Camargo was reportedly carrying the bloody clitoris and clothes of his latest victim along with a copy of Dostoyevsky's *Crime and Punishment* when he was arrested. In custody, he confessed to the rape and murder of 72 girls in Ecuador. In all, estimates put Camargo's victim count as high as 150.

Camargo was sentenced to 16 years, the maximum allowed under Ecuadorian law, but never reached the end of his term. A fellow prisoner killed him in 1994.

Q: Who is the Colombian "Beast" who confessed to nearly 150 murders?

A: Luis Garavito blamed his own abusive childhood, which included torture and rape, for his horrendous murders of as many as 182 young boys in Colombia in the 1990s.

Garavito kept a notebook of victims, which totaled 140 at the time of his arrest and dated to 1992. *La Bestia* (the Beast) targeted the children of street vendors who had been left unattended as well as young homeless boys whose presence wouldn't be missed. He tied up his victims, mutilated them, and slit their throats.

After Garavito was arrested in 1999, Colombian investigators claimed he had variously posed as a monk, an indigent, a street vendor, and even as a representative of fake foundations for elderly and children's charities.

One of Colombia's worst serial killers in history received several lengthy prison sentences totaling more than 800 years, but the maximum time anyone can serve in Colombia is 60 years (until recently, it was only 40). In 2011 a Colombian politician stoked public fear that Garavito could soon be released because he completed "study hours" that would reduce his sentence. Prison Director Gustavo Adolfo Ricaurte assured the public, however, that Garavito wasn't going anywhere, noting that the mass killer still has another 25 cases pending against him in Colombia, and Ecuador has also sentenced him to 22 years for murders there.

Q: Where is Pedro Alonso López, another killer with connections to Colombia and Ecuador?

A: No one seems to know.

The Monster of the Andes began targeting young girls in Peru in the 1970s after his release from prison, where he had served time for stealing cars and selling off their parts. In total, López eventually confessed to raping and murdering about 300 young girls across Peru, Colombia, and Ecuador.

The world was almost rid of this dude when the elders of Ayacucho decided to execute him for his crimes against young members of the native Peruvian tribe. An American missionary stepped in and convinced them to spare his life, however, and López was turned over to the police—who released him.

López then moved on to Colombia and Ecuador, sometimes killing at a rate of three girls a week, he later said. He reportedly preferred committing his crimes in the daylight so he could better watch his victims suffering, and especially see the look in their eyes as he strangled them.

When a flood near Ambato in Ecuador uncovered the bodies of four missing girls in 1980, police and citizens were on high alert. So when López attempted to lure a 12-year-old girl away from her mother at an open-air market, the mother and other members of the public chased him down and held him until the police arrived.

López served out a full 16-year term in Ecuador and was then deported to Colombia, where he was placed in a psychiatric facility as he was judged insane. In 1998 he was declared sane and released.

Since then, there's been nary a word on the whereabouts of Pedro Alonso López, arguably one of the worst serial killers in South American history.

Q: What bedtime story may have led Ukrainian killer Andrei Chikatilo to cannibalism?

A: When Chikatilo was a young boy in a Ukrainian farming village, his mother repeatedly told him that his older brother had been kidnapped, murdered, and eaten by neighbors during the famine that ravaged Russia in the 1930s. This may partly explain how the Rostov Ripper came to be.

Described as a "shy, bookish, nearsighted, effeminate bed-wetter" by the New York Daily News, Chikatilo was ridiculed as a child and even as an adult, when as a teacher he had extreme difficulty speaking in front of his class. He was married and, although mostly impotent, fathered two children.

Chikatilo's first victim was nine-year-old Lena Zakotnova; in December of 1978 he raped, strangled, and stabbed her over and over. He got away with it, though, because ex-convict Alexsandr Kravchenko, age 25, was beaten into a confession and was tried, convicted, and executed for this crime.

Soon after he murdered Zakotnova, Chikatilo was fired from his teaching job for spying on student bathrooms; then he was fired from another job for similar reasons. He landed at a boarding school in charge of the boys' dormitory, and within months he was fired for trying to molest a student. Then he got a job as a supply clerk that involved travel, enabling him to move around Russia and expand his pool of potential victims, focusing on bus and train stations.

Chikatilo was particularly brutal, carving up victims' bodies, especially their genitals and eyes. Some victims had their tongues removed, and others were dissected. During his confession, he detailed how he drank the blood or ate body parts of victims to finish off the murders.

Chikatilo narrowly escaped from police suspicion several times during his killing of 53 to 56 women and young girls and boys throughout Russia. In a particularly frustrating miss in 1984, authorities zeroed in on the gray-haired Chikatilo after he was caught fondling a sleeping girl on a bench at a bus station. They searched his briefcase and found rope, a knife, and petroleum jelly. Still, they let him go because his blood type didn't match that of the purported killer—a discrepancy that has never been adequately explained.

At first repentant of his crimes, pointing to a childhood in which he was "unable to realize myself as a real man and a complete human being," Chikatilo later changed to acting insane during court proceedings. He appeared as a wide-eyed "Slavic Charles Manson," even flashing his "useless" private parts and shouting, "I am a mistake of nature, a mad beast!"

Communist propaganda that serial murder simply didn't exist in a "people's republic" is largely blamed for Chikatilo's long reign of terror. Indeed, he was released one time after officials intervened and alleged that a party member was being persecuted.

Chikatilo was executed in 1994 with one shot to the back of his head.

Q: What did Ahmad Suradji do with victims' bodies because he thought it gave him power?

A: The Indonesian killer buried his victims with their heads pointing toward his home in order to channel the power of their spirits.

Yeah, let's back up on this one.

Suradji was a self-proclaimed sorcerer—also known as Datuk or Nasib Kelawang—who lived near Medan, the capital of North Sumatra. In 1986 his father appeared to him in a dream, he said, and told him to drink the saliva of 70 women to gain status as a mystic healer. In his confession, Suradji noted that his father didn't instruct him to kill—the murders were his own spin on the dream, designed to help him meet his objective faster.

As far as murderous plots, Suradji was set up nicely. He was already offering spiritual advice and selling black magic items from his home, so it wasn't unusual for women to show up looking for guidance. From there, he could upsell to performing rituals for beauty, wealth, a lover's fidelity, and so on.

The victim would pay a fee of $200 to $400 for Suradji to bury her up to her waist in his nearby sugarcane plantation as part of the ritual. But then he would strangle her with a cord, drink her saliva, strip off her clothes, and bury her with her head pointing toward his house.

In 1997, after a search for one missing young woman led authorities to Suradji's plantation because eyewitnesses had seen her traveling there, his murderous ways were slowly revealed through excavations.

He confessed to being responsible for the deaths of 42 women, ranging from teenagers to 40 years of age.

Suradji's three wives—who were sisters—were arrested for helping him, but only Tumini was tried and convicted as an accomplice. She received a sentence of life imprisonment.

Suradji was sentenced to death by firing squad, which took place in 2008.

Q: What member of Chinese royalty was one of the earliest serial killers on record?

A: Liu Pengli, a son of King Xiao of Liang, was named the king of Jidong in 144 BC by his cousin, Emperor Jing. In what is truly an egregious understatement, Pengli abused his power as king as he instituted his own ancient, twisted version of *The Hunger Games* among his own people—terrorizing them, hunting them down, and using a band of slaves to kill them.

This went on for nearly 20 years, until the son of one of Pengli's victims ratted him out to Emperor Jing—but not before the body count added up to around 100.

Although execution was considered, his cousin showed Pengli mercy and merely stripped him of his title and exiled him from the kingdom.

History didn't record anything about Pengli after that, so there's no telling whether his serial killing stopped when his power was taken away.

Q: What killings became the subject of the British miniseries *Rillington Place*?

A: John Reginald Halliday Christie's crimes went undetected until he moved out of his London flat at 10 Rillington Place in 1953 and the new tenant found a hollow spot in the kitchen wall. He tore down the wallpaper, pulled away a loose panel, and saw a woman's body curled up in the old coal storage space. Further investigation revealed three decomposing female bodies, each wrapped in a blanket tied with thick string and electric wire.

The body of Christie's wife Ethel was discovered under the dining room floorboards, and the bones of two additional victims were found buried in the garden. In all, Christie killed at least eight women, favoring prostitutes, and kept souvenir tins of pubic hair—some of which didn't match any of his known victims.

Christie, whose friends called him Reg, suffered from impotence but found strangling women arousing. Once they were dead he would rape them. His first victim was Ruth Fuerst, in 1943; he strangled her during sex and buried her body in the garden.

When his neighbor, an illiterate alcoholic named Timothy Evans, told police in 1949 that he had concealed the body of his wife Beryl in a drain, police searched and eventually found her corpse and the body of their infant daughter, Geraldine, in a shed behind the three-story house. Both had been strangled. Disturbingly, Christie talked with detectives in his garden as his dog dug about and uncovered a skull, which Christie nonchalantly covered back up while holding court with the detectives. They didn't even notice.

Evans at first confessed to murdering his wife and daughter but later claimed that she had died while Christie was performing an illegal abortion on her. He said he didn't know what had happened to his daughter. Nonetheless, Evans was convicted and hanged for the murders.

On trial himself several years later, Christie failed to convince a jury of his insanity and was sentenced to death in the gallows. He was hanged in 1953.

Rillington Place, released in 2016 on BBC One, recounts this grisly tale in three parts, each told from the perspective of a different main character: Christie, his wife Ethel, and Evans.

Q: What Mexican city gained a reputation as a serial killer's playground in the 1990s?

A: Ciudad Juárez is the most populous city in the Mexican state of Chihuahua and is just across the border from El Paso, Texas. In 2005, Amnesty International estimated that since 1993 more than 370 young women and girls had been murdered in the city and throughout Chihuahua; a third of them also suffered sexual violence. And that doesn't include the number of women still missing.

The area has long been known for its drug trade and police corruption, and no one truly believes that all of those murder victims can be attributed to just one serial killer. But the Juárez Ripper, alternately called the Strangler, is considered to be among the culprits.

The first victim linked to the Ripper was Alma Chavira Farel, whose beaten, raped, and strangled body was found in the Campestre Virreyes district on January 23, 1993. Police recorded another 16 slayings that same year, all occurring in similar ways. Some also had slash marks across their breasts, giving the Ripper his name. Eight women were murdered the following year, and by mid-September of 1995 another 19 women were dead.

Police pinpointed suspect Abdel Latif Sharif, an Egyptian chemist who had emigrated to the United States in the 1970s. Sharif had committed multiple horrible acts against women, including rape, for which he served five years of a 12-year prison sentence before receiving early parole. Several years later he held a woman captive in his home in Texas and raped her; his attorney convinced prosecutors to drop the charges in exchange for Sharif's leaving the country for good. And so he ended up in Juárez.

Sharif was convicted of the 1995 murder of 17-year-old Elizabeth Castro Garcia, but murders continued even after he was in custody. Then police turned to blaming a street gang called *Los Rebeldes* (the Rebels) as being in cahoots with Sharif in the Garcia murder and 16 others. That explanation soon fell apart, and over the years the police have explored several other theories. Those have involved organ harvesters, satanic cults, wealthy sadists, police officers, and the city's ubiquitous drug cartels.

Many Juárez victims had their hands bound behind them with a shoelace and were strangled, and some had shoes neatly placed behind their partially naked bodies. The murdered young women generally had shoulder-length hair and were poor, dark-complexioned, and thin. Many bodies were impossible to identify because of their extensive injuries and advanced decomposition.

Lourdes Portrillo's documentary *Señorita Extraviada* (*Missing Young Woman*), which won a special jury prize at the 2002 Sundance Festival, explores the Ciudad Juárez murders in depth. Still, it doesn't appear that anyone is close to solving the vast majority of killings committed in this "serial killer's playground," strewn with far too many pink crosses planted in remembrance of dead women.

Another potential suspect is serial killer Alejandro Máynez, who has murdered at least two women but possibly as many as 50. Sharif himself has pointed to Máynez as the Ripper.

Q: Who is the Bikini Killer noted for escaping from high-security prisons? Yes, plural.

A: Charles Sobhraj, who committed as many as a dozen murders in the 1970s, got his nickname because many of his victims were found wearing bikinis. He was also known as the Serpent because he repeatedly slipped past the authorities—even from inside prison.

Sobhraj was of Indian and Vietnamese descent but grew up in France, which he didn't enjoy as he was bullied for being different from the other children.

As a criminal Sobhraj delighted in targeting wealthy tourists, and so the Hippie Trail in Southeast Asia became a favorite spot. Described as flashy and handsome, he charmed his way into many situations and was able to extract himself from others—such as jail. One of his favorite methods of escaping prison walls was pretending to be ill and then drugging the guard.

He jetted from country to country (often using stolen passports), stealing to finance his travels. He also left a trail of dead bodies, including American tourist Teresa Knowlton from Seattle, found drowned in a tidal pool in the Gulf of Thailand in 1975. Sobhraj had murdered her at his apartment, then had an accomplice dispose of her body.

Sobhraj strangled some victims, and in one particularly ambitious scheme he drugged a class of 60 French students, intending to rob them. Instead, enough members fell ill to warrant emergency room visits, foiling his plan.

This veritable international man of mystery served time for murder in India from 1976 to 1997, and upon release he returned to France and became a celebrity criminal. He appeared on talk shows, granted interviews, and otherwise used his charm and good looks to profit from his crimes.

But then he landed in Nepal, and police came looking for him on open warrants for two 1975 murders. The case files had been lost, but that didn't stop the prosecution. In 2004 Sobhraj was convicted by the Kathmandu district court and sentenced to life imprisonment. All his appeals have failed—as have any attempts he may have made to escape this time around. In early 2019, the Nepalese government was considering whether Sobhraj is eligible for early release under the country's Senior Citizens Act, which can waive remaining prison time for some offenders.

Q: Who was the illiterate farm worker tried, convicted, and later absolved as Italy's Monster of Florence?

A: Pietro Pacciani.

The Monster of Florence killed 16 people—eight man/woman couples—in lovers' lanes in the Tuscan countryside between 1968 and 1985. Generally the perpetrator approached couples in cars on moonless nights and either shot or stabbed them. In some instances, the woman's genitals and/or breasts were removed by the killer, who wore rubber surgical gloves and may have used a scalpel.

Il Mostro di Firenze is Italy's most notorious serial killer, largely because few people are satisfied with the theory that a group of men—*compagni di merende*, or snack buddies, as the court called them—carried out the crimes. Pacciani was tried and convicted of the murders only to have his conviction overturned in 1996. An ex-con, Pacciani had already served 13 years for murdering a man he had caught with his ex-girlfriend.

Although a retrial was planned, Pacciani died just as his three alleged accomplices—Giovanni Faggi, Giancarlo Lotti, and Mario Vanni—went on trial in 1997. Faggi was acquitted, while Vanni and Lotti were convicted. Vanni got life in prison, while Lotti received a 26-year sentence.

All four men were from the island of Sardinia, leading authorities to characterize them as a kind of Sardinian gang. That theory was later expanded on by Detective Michele Giuttari, who also raised the specter of a satanic cult's involvement.

The killer taunted police with a letter in 1982 and another in 1985, directed to prosecutor Silvia Della Monica. The second letter included the severed nipple of a victim and so rattled Della Monica that she left her position not long thereafter.

In what would be one of the most bizarre aspects of any serial killer case if true, the Monster may actually have carried his first female victim's six-year-old son to safety after killing his mother and her lover. Barbara Locci's son Natalino was sleeping in the back seat of the car during the murders, but he ended up at a nearby house seeking help. Natalino first said he had been carried there but then said he had walked—a story detectives doubted, since the boy wasn't wearing shoes.

In 2018 a new theory emerged into the mainstream, that the Zodiac Killer and the Monster of Florence were one and the same: Italian-American Joe Bevilacqua, custodian of an American military cemetery in Tuscany.

In sum: this case is destined to remain one of the most befuddling, convoluted, and mysterious of all serial killer tales.

Q: Who are Canada's infamous Ken and Barbie serial killers?

A: Husband and wife Paul Bernardo and Karla Homolka, named the Ken and Barbie killers for their (arguable) resemblance to the plastic dolls, defied the friendly Canadian stereotype big time.

The couple's first victim was Homolka's 15-year-old sister Tammy, who died on Christmas Eve in 1990. Bernardo drugged Tammy's drinks after dinner, and once she was out he videotaped Karla performing oral sex on her sister. Then he raped her as Karla held a cloth doused in an animal tranquilizer (from the veterinary clinic where she worked) over the girl's mouth. Tammy threw up from the drug, aspirated her own vomit, and died. The death didn't look suspicious to outsiders, though, and was ruled accidental.

This occurred, by the way, five months after Homolka allegedly facilitated Bernardo's rape of Tammy by lacing her dinner with Valium to knock her out.

Over the course of the next 16 months the couple kidnapped two teenagers, 14-year-old Leslie Mahaffy and 15-year-old Kirsten French. Then they raped, sodomized, otherwise sexually tortured, and murdered them—and videotaped it. Mahaffy suffered an entire night of terror; French was tortured over three days.

The couple cut Mahaffy's body into pieces, formed cement blocks around them, and then dumped them into Lake Gibson. One of the blocks was discovered two weeks later.

After DNA evidence linked Bernardo to the crime scenes, Homolka confessed, and the two were arrested in 1993. Homolka cooperated with prosecutors, claiming she had also been a victim of Bernardo's violence and wasn't a willing participant in the crimes. She received just 12 years in prison in exchange for pleading guilty to manslaughter. Bernardo was convicted of murder and was sentenced to life in prison with a designation as a dangerous offender, making his chances of parole unlikely.

Remember those videotapes, though? Yeah, they popped up after Homolka had reached her plea bargain and told a far different story from the one she had been spinning. She seemed to be more involved in the crimes than she had let on, which led to Canadian headlines such as "Deal with the Devil."

Homolka was released from prison in 2005.

Q: What Macedonian crime reporter became a serial killer himself?

A: Vlado Taneski gave himself away as the murderer of three elderly cleaning ladies when he included details in his articles that only the killer would know, since the police hadn't made them public.

Once authorities grew suspicious, they matched his DNA with semen from the crime scenes. Taneski had left his victims naked, bound with telephone cables, and stuffed into bags. All of the reporter's victims lived close to him and shared similarities with his mother, with whom he had a strained relationship. Taneski's father had died by suicide in 1990.

His mother even knew the women: 65-year-old Zivana Temelkoska, 56-year-old Ljubica Licoska, and 64-year-old Mitra Simjanoska. Police also suspected Taneski in the 2003 disappearance of a 78-year-old woman.

His motivations and the extent of his crimes will likely never be known, however. Prison officials found the journalist face down in a bucket of water in his jail cell where he was being held with two other inmates after his 2008 arrest.

Q: What brutal Japanese serial killer bayonetted a pregnant woman?

A: By his own account, while stationed in China as a Japanese soldier in the late 1920s Yoshio Kodaira and four or five colleagues entered the home of a civilian family, tied up the father, and locked him in a closet while they robbed the family and raped the women. They finished off by cutting the fetus from the womb of one young woman.

Kodaira was discharged from the military after several women accused him of assault. Post-military he got married, but the union didn't last long. When his wife returned to her family, Kodaira showed up and killed his father-in-law with an iron bar, also injuring six other family members.

He served five years of hard labor for that crime, and upon his release in 1940 he married again, had a son, and worked as a boilerman at a naval depot in Tokyo. In 1945, after forming a friendship with 19-year-old Miyazaki Mitsuko, the married man expressed his love for her. When she rejected him for being too old for her, he raped and strangled her and then hid her body in an air shelter.

Mitsuko's body went undiscovered for six weeks because American planes weren't conducting any bombings during that time. After his eventual arrest in 1946, Kodaira shared his logic that he knew he would be caught for the murder of Mitsuko but could only be sentenced to die once, and "there were many young girls who attracted me." And so his killing had continued.

Kodaira targeted young women on their way to market to buy food, so he would rob them in addition to assaulting and killing them—eight more victims in addition to Mitsuko. He claimed he used their money to buy food for the less fortunate.

Kodaira's mistake came when he told a new acquaintance, 17-year-old Ryuko Midorikawa, his real name before arranging to meet her one day to take her to a job interview. Ryuko disappeared, and her parents knew exactly where to send police.

As he had predicted, Kodaira was sentenced to death and then hanged at Miyagi Prison in 1949.

Q: How did the "Tehran vampire" lure his victims?

A: The 28-year-old Iranian serial killer Ali Reza Khoshruy Kuran Kordiyeh posed as a taxi driver to get women into his car and then abduct, rape, and stab them to death. To inhibit identification of the bodies, he burned them.

Kordiyeh confessed to victimizing nine girls and women, ranging in age from 10 to 47, in the span of just a few months in 1997. His victims included a mother and daughter.

After Iranian officials made the rare move of leaking the location of his execution, the spectacle drew a sporting event–like crowd of 10,000 to 20,000 people, including the victims' families.

In the same neighborhood where he had stalked for victims, Kordiyeh was hung from a construction crane suspended above the spectators—but not before one male relative of each victim whipped him with a thick leather belt as he lay tied to a metal bed. Those lashes were part of Kordiyeh's total sentence of 214; the others had been delivered by prison officials earlier that week.

Iranian authorities certainly weren't messing around with Kordiyeh's punishment, but it still wasn't as severe as the families would have preferred. They had advocated death by stoning, and that his hands to be cut off first since he was allegedly also a thief.

Q: What German killer said his greatest thrill would be to hear blood spurt from his own neck?

A: From beginning to end, the story of the Peter Kürten—called the Monster of Düsseldorf and the Vampire of Düsseldorf—ranks among the most disturbing in serial killer annals. And he certainly had a thing about blood.

The tale begins with Kürten's birth in 1883 and an abusive childhood that featured an alcoholic father who beat his children and wife, also forcing his wife to strip naked so they could have sex in front of the children in their one-room apartment. Kürten's father was later convicted of incest with his daughter, and Kürten himself attempted to have sex with his sisters.

The neighbors apparently weren't much better. As a young boy, Kürten developed a bond with a bestiality-prone dogcatcher who lived in the same building, and Kürten began performing sexual acts with dogs himself. As he got older, he expanded his experiences to include sex with farm animals such as sheep, pigs, and goats, and realized that his pleasure was heightened if he stabbed the animal just before he reached orgasm.

Kürten claims that his first murders occurred when he was nine years old and pushed a schoolmate who couldn't swim off a pier. When another friend jumped in to save him, Kürten held his head under water until he drowned. Both deaths were ruled accidental.

When Kürten left home as an early teen, he began a life of petty crime, stealing to survive. He claimed that he strangled a girl during sex in

1899, though no body was ever found. He served time for theft and was drafted into the military upon his release, but he deserted; he also served time for that.

By the time he sexually assaulted and murdered 13-year-old Christine Klein in 1913, Kürten had become a rapist and an arsonist. According to his own account, he poisoned several fellow inmates as he served time for theft again.

Kürten earned his nicknames during a nine-month span in 1929 when he murdered at least nine people and attacked several others. His obsession with blood carries through all of the murders. He stabbed one elderly victim 24 times with razor-sharp scissors and stabbed a nine-year-old girl in the genitals, among other areas, while he was ejaculating. He then inserted his semen into her vagina with his fingers. He also drank the blood of a few victims, once to the point of vomiting—earning him his "vampire" nickname.

Kürten confessed to many more crimes than the police had connected him to—68 in all, including 10 murders—but he was tried on nine counts of murder and seven counts of attempted murder. He pleaded insanity, but jurors didn't buy it. They convicted him within 90 minutes of deliberation. Kürten smiled all the way to the guillotine in 1931.

Dr. Karl Berg, one of five experts who testified at Kürten's trial that he was sane, called him "the king of sexual perverts." That is a description that's hard to argue with.

Q: Who was South Africa's ABC killer?

A: In 1997 Moses Sithole was convicted of 40 rapes and 38 killings, called the ABC murders because he began in July of 1994 in Atteridgeville, moved on to Boksburg, and ended in Cleveland in October of 1995.

In early October 1995, Sithole called a Johannesburg newspaper claiming he had killed 76 women to avenge a 14-year prison sentence he'd served for a rape he said he didn't commit. The situation was so dire that President Nelson Mandela pleaded directly with the public for help in capturing the ABC killer.

Creepily enough, Sithole was a youth counselor with a faux charity called Youth Against Human Abuse, which he used as a cover to lure his victims, often with promises of work. He would then beat, rape, and strangle them with their underwear or other articles of their own clothing. He left their bodies in desolate fields, at train stations, and at mining sites.

Of the women he raped and killed, he said to an interviewer, "I have taught them a very good lesson."

During his arrest in October 1995, Sithole wounded two officers with an axe before they subdued him by shooting him in the stomach and foot. When he finally faced trial in December 1997 he was convicted and sentenced to a total of 2,410 years in prison—with the possibility of parole after 930 years.

Q: Who was Hungary's Grinning Tinsmith of Cinkota?

A: Bela Kiss was the Hungarian serial killer who sealed his victims in large tin drums—and never faced legal repercussions for his crimes.

A ladies' man, pleasant and likable, Kiss never bothered his neighbors in the Hungarian village of Cinkota. Yet he murdered several of his female lovers and deposited their bodies in handmade tin drums.

Kiss had left a stack of letters from women with his housekeeper, Frau Jakubek, which she was to give to authorities if he died in battle after being called to serve in World War I. He had apparently been placing newspaper advertisements to draw women to his home with empty promises of marriage, and he had received quite a collection of responses, including some from the United States.

In a contemporaneous article, the *Washington Post* called Bela Kiss the Hungarian Bluebeard, and his tale achieved legendary status the longer Kiss remained at large. His victim number has been cited at somewhere between six and 24. In some versions the drums were buried and dug up by family members of the missing women, while in others his landlord found them in a storeroom after Kiss went to war. Another version says soldiers hoping to find gasoline during the war were led to Kiss's property but found bodies instead. Some tales say one of the barrels was full of women's clothes.

In newspaper accounts, Kiss was described alternately as "a handsome young blade" when he arrived in Cinkota as a young man, and "very much like a gorilla." Sometimes he was said to have a yellow beard, and sometimes it was red. In sum, it's difficult to get a grip on how much of what's out there about Kiss is factual.

And then there's the matter of his death. At the time the bodies were discovered, authorities believed Kiss had died in the war, either on the battlefield or from typhoid in a Serbian prison. Periodically thereafter the media would report that Kiss had been located: once in a Romanian prison under the assumed identity of soldier Franz Wimer, and another time as a well-liked French citizen—still a tinsmith, mind you—living in Oran, Algiers, with his wife and children.

In any event, Kiss was never arrested for the murders, and he remains one of Hungary's worst serial killers.

Q: What brought Austrian serial killer Jack Unterweger to Los Angeles in 1992?

A: An Austrian magazine commissioned Unterweger to write about (wait for it …) crime, and they sent him to Los Angeles to do so. Thus he was able to expand his penchant for murdering prostitutes across the pond.

Unterweger's story is one of failed redemption. The son of an Austrian prostitute and an American soldier, he grew up among women in the sex trade. He developed such a hatred for them that he strangled a sex worker with her bra and was convicted of murder in 1974, when he was 25 years old.

When asked about the motive behind his crime, Unterweger said, "I envisioned my mother in front of me, and I killed her."

This is where Unterweger's story could have started to turn around, as he became a widely respected author while in prison—so much so that authorities decided he was rehabilitated and should be released in 1990. For several months Unterweger relished a flashy lifestyle full of television appearances and expensive clothes and cars, except he also kept killing. Six Austrian prostitutes were found murdered during this time.

Then in 1991, Unterweger jumped at the chance to travel to the United States for "work," and he even arranged ride-alongs with the Los Angeles Police Department as part of his "research" on street crime. Meanwhile, three local prostitutes were strangled with their bras.

By the time LA police caught on to Unterweger he was back in Austria, where authorities were already closing in on him for the murders there. But Unterweger disappeared with his young girlfriend, traveling to Switzerland, Paris, and New York before landing in Miami, where he was arrested in 1992. He was extradited to Austria and tried and convicted on 11 counts of murder, including the three in Los Angeles.

In 1994, just hours after he was sentenced, Unterweger hanged himself from a curtain rod in his prison cell with the string from his jogging pants.

Q: What serial killer worked as a butler for the British aristocracy as he thieved and murdered in the 1970s?

A: In the case of Scottish serial killer Archibald Thomson Hall, the butler really did do it. Hall murdered five people, including a former politician, and was sentenced to life imprisonment.

As a young man, Hall wisely used his period of incarceration for attempting to sell stolen jewelry to brush up on aristocratic etiquette and tone down his thick Scottish accent. Upon his release, he settled on the flashier name Roy Fontaine (inspired by Hollywood actress Joan Fontaine) and sought work as a butler, using forged references. He aimed high because the wealthy would have the finest jewelry, of course.

After years of petty crime, in the mid-1970s Hall graduated to murder. He had procured a job for ex-con friend David Wright, working with him at the estate of Lady Peggy Hudson, but an argument ensued between the two. Some reports suggest that Wright threatened to expose Hall's criminal past if he did not carry through with a plan to steal from Lady Hudson with him. Others say Wright had stolen from Lady Hudson, which angered Hall because he was loyal to her and was trying to go straight. Whatever the core of the disagreement, Wright ended up buried near a stream on the property.

Not long after, Hall was working for Mr. and Mrs. Walter Travers Scott-Elliott, he an 82-year-old former Labour MP and she 20 years younger. One night Hall invited another thief, Michael Kitto, to admire the items they could pilfer, but Mrs. Scott-Elliott caught them at it. The pair killed her but then had the problem of Mr. Scott-Elliott, who was also home.

The next day, they drugged the old man to get him out of the house and into the car, and then they put his wife's body in the trunk. A third accomplice, Mary Coggle, dressed as Mrs. Scott-Elliott (including her $4,000 mink coat) and traveled with them to Perthshire to dispose of Mrs. Scott-Elliott's body. The husband was then killed as well, and his body discarded.

Unhappy with Coggle's behavior—she hardly ever took off the mink coat and swiped handfuls of jewelry from the Scott-Elliott house—the men killed her, too.

Hall's final victim was his half-brother, Donald Hall, who was asking too many questions about the pair's exploits. Hall and accomplice Kitto were arrested when they stopped at a hotel on the way to dispose of Donald's body, still in the trunk. The hotel proprietor thought them a bit too chatty and called the police to check things out. Upon discovering that the car had stolen tags, they took the duo into custody—and found the body in the trunk.

In 2002 the Monster Butler died of natural causes at the age of 78 in prison.

Q: Who was the Yorkshire Ripper?

A: Peter Sutcliffe, who wore a V-neck sweater inverted under his pants to expose his genitals, killed at least 13 women in West Yorkshire, England before he was arrested in 1981. He had been pulled over by police and found to have a fake license plate and a prostitute in the car with him. Authorities nearly let him slip away when he asked to relieve himself around the corner. The killer didn't run, but he did dump a hammer, rope, and knife, which were found the next day and eventually helped link him to the brutal Ripper murders.

Police discovered Sutcliffe's interesting wardrobe choice of the V-neck sweater under his pants during a strip search at the station.

Two days after his arrest, Sutcliffe confessed to killing 13 women, all prostitutes, adding that God had told him do so. Sutcliffe's weapon of choice was a hammer, with which he would bash victims' skulls. He also stabbed them with a sharpened screwdriver and a knife.

During the Ripper investigation, the police received letters and a tape from someone claiming to be the perpetrator. Once Sutcliffe was captured, though, it became clear that the correspondence was a hoax, as Sutcliffe's voice and handwriting didn't match. No one was ever identified as the fake Ripper.

Sutcliffe attempted to plead diminished capacity, but the judge rejected his plea and he was found guilty on all 13 counts of murder. He was sentenced to life imprisonment without parole and was later placed in Broadmoor Hospital, a high-security mental health facility in Berkshire.

During incarceration Sutcliffe has sustained several injuries inflicted by fellow inmates, including the loss of vision in one eye—perhaps symbolic as Sutcliffe had stabbed one victim's corpse in the eye because of its "reproachful stare."

Q: What common household problem led to the arrest of Germany's Duisburg Man-Eater?

A: A clogged toilet was the only "common" part about Joachim Kroll's problem, as what was stopping up his commode was human organs. Kroll had mentioned to a neighbor in passing that his toilet was stopped up with guts, which didn't mean much until police went door to door in 1976 searching for information about missing four-year-old Marion Ketter. The comment made police look more closely at Kroll, and they made the gruesome discovery of human flesh bagged up in the freezer and Ketter's tiny hand cooking on the stove in a pot with carrots and potatoes.

Kroll, who was also called the Ruhr Hunter, eventually confessed to killing 14 people, mostly young girls, often raping and mutilating their corpses and then eating parts of some. Kroll also liked to masturbate over the battered and bloody bodies, once leaving so much semen on the face and genitals that authorities believed there must have been more than one attacker. He regularly sliced off pieces of victims' bodies and prepared them like steaks. Immediately following his murders he would return home for sex with a rubber doll as he relived his crimes.

Perhaps unsurprising in light of how creepy Kroll's actions were in general, the man called "Uncle Joachim" by neighborhood kids kept child-sized dolls on which he would carry out practice runs, choking them while he masturbated.

Kroll's murderous spree lasted more than 20 years. He avoided detection for so long partly because several other men were tried for his crimes. One even confessed to the 1959 murder of 15-year-old

Manuela Knodt and, despite recanting later, was sentenced to eight years in prison. In an especially tragic turn of events, Adolf Schickel jumped off a bridge because he couldn't take the pressure of the accusations levied against him regarding the death of his girlfriend, 20-year-old Ursula Rohling, whom Kroll had murdered in 1966.

Kroll was man of small stature and an IQ that placed him well below average. His motive for the killings and cannibalism, he said, was to keep his grocery bills down.

After a 151-day trial he received a sentence of life in prison, where he died of a heart attack in 1991.

Q: What killer changed his name in honor of a kung fu movie star?

A: England's Bruce Lee is the former Peter George Dinsdale, born in 1960. A raging pyromanic, Lee once pledged allegiance to fire: "Fire is my master," he said, "and that is why I cause these fires."

Born with epilepsy, Lee had a noticeable limp in his right leg, a deformed arm, and seeming mental deficiencies; locals called him Daft Peter. His pyromanic ways weren't discovered until a 1979 fire at the Hastie home on Selby Street in Hull, England, which killed mother Edith and her three sons.

The Hasties weren't well liked in the neighborhood, so authorities had a long list of suspects. Lee made it easy for them, though, when he casually confessed to setting the fire. He claimed that he had been sexually involved with one of the residents, who was blackmailing him.

And then Lee kept talking.

He confessed to a series of fires that had killed 26 people in the 1970s. In 1981, at age 20, he pleaded guilty to manslaughter in those deaths and was placed in a high-security psychiatric hospital. A nursing home fire that had caused 11 fatalities and that he had taken credit for was later determined to be accidental, so Lee was cleared of those deaths.

Q: What Japanese killer sparked a movement to restrict pornographic videos?

A: Tsutomu Miyazaki was 26 years old in 1989 when he was arrested for the abduction and murder of four girls, ages four to seven, in a Tokyo suburb. He raped their corpses and drank the blood of one victim, ate part of the hands of two, slept next to the dead girls, and wrote taunting letters to the media and the victims' families. Miyazaki burned the body of one victim and left the remains on her parents' doorstep.

A search of his room revealed nearly 6,000 videotapes of horror and anime films; one of the murders followed the plot of a film called *Flower of Blood and Flesh*, in which a young woman has her head and wrists cut off with a knife and saw. His collection of films, coupled with his appalling acts, led to much criticism of the Japanese fascination with *rori-kon*, or Lolita complex, the sexual attraction to prepubescent girls.

Miyazaki alternately claimed that a "rat man" was responsible for the atrocities—he even drew a cartoonish figure of said rat man—and that he had committed the crimes to "satisfy his necrophiliac fantasies."

Miyazaki's father, unable to cope with what his son had done, died by suicide in 1994, to which the killer responded, "I feel refreshed." He was hanged in 2008.

Q: Who was the Cul-de-Sac Killer, said to have a pathological hatred of the elderly?

A: Stephen Akinmurele was just 20 years old when he was arrested for the murders of five pensioners between the years of 1995 and 1998—Eric and Joan Boardman and former landlady Jemmimah Cargill in Blackpool, England, and Dorothy Harris and Marjorie Ashton on the Isle of Man. All of his victims lived in culs-de-sac, giving him his nickname.

The female victims were all strangled, but Eric Boardman was bludgeoned to death with a thick, heavy stick while trying to defend his wife. Fingerprints on the weapon linked Akinmurele to the crime, and authorities believed the young man might have been linked to an additional 10 murders.

Akinmurele never faced a trial or confessed to any more killings, however, as he hanged himself in his Manchester prison cell in 1999 while on suicide watch. In his suicide note, he expressed both regret for his actions and the fear that he would kill again.

Q: What British killer do some believe responsible for the crimes of Bible John?

A: In May 2007, Peter Tobin was convicted for the murder of 23-year-old Angelika Kluk, a student who had been cleaning St. Patrick's Roman Catholic Church in Glasgow. Her body was found under the confessional, and she had been raped, beaten, and stabbed. Tobin, the last person seen with her, received a life sentence for the crimes.

Several months later, two bodies turned up in Tobin's garden in Margate, Kent, and he was convicted for the murders of Vicky Hamilton, age 15, and Dinah McNicol, 18. He received two additional life sentences for those deaths, now without the possibility of parole.

Tobin is widely suspected to be Bible John, an unidentified serial killer of three women between February 1968 and October 1969 in Glasgow. All of the women were raped and strangled after attending the Barrowland Ballroom. The perpetrator was called Bible John because, rather predictably, he said his name was John and he quoted from the Bible.

Tobin, who was known to frequent that location, matched the physical description one witness gave of Bible John, and the murders stopped when Tobin met his wife at the ballroom and left Glasgow for good. The killing methods also overlapped with those of the later murders.

Moreover, Tobin's ex-wives claimed he had raped and beaten them, and he had spent time with the Jesus Fellowship in Coventry, attempting to hide from charges of previous rapes and attempted murders. He was caught and convicted, by the way, and served eight years of a 14-year-sentence—all before the murders for which he was eventually put away. Tobin also had had a tooth extracted, right where one witness said Bible John was missing one.

In what is perhaps the oddest tidbit of the whole ordeal, all of Bible John's victims were menstruating at the time of their deaths and had tampons or pads placed near them—perhaps not terribly strange in itself, except that his wives said Tobin had a particular aversion to women's menstrual cycles—quite a coincidence.

In 2015 Tobin was viciously attacked by a fellow inmate, child rapist Sean Moynihan, leaving him with a facial scar from a razor blade slice. By early 2019, the convicted murderer who had once cut a victim's body in half was so frail from cancer that he could no longer leave his cell.

Tobin will likely die with his secrets, but he did confess to a prison psychiatrist that he had killed 48 women in all—and then added with a smile, "Prove it."

Q: What UK killer embodied the stereotype of a creepy man luring little girls into a van?

A: Scottish-born Robert Black was a delivery driver in north London who used his van as a traveling murder scene as he kidnapped, raped, and murdered at least four young girls in the 1980s. He is suspected in as many as 14 other child disappearances and/or murders throughout several countries, including the UK, Ireland, Germany, France, and the Netherlands.

Young Robert was bullied and nicknamed Smelly Bob for his lack of personal hygiene—and then he turned into a bully himself. At the age of 12 he sexually assaulted a young girl in a public bathroom, and throughout his adolescence he exhibited inappropriate sexualized behavior toward other children. He claimed that as a 15-year-old delivery boy for the local butcher he had fondled up to 40 girls in their homes.

Black's four confirmed victims, murdered between 1981 and 1986, were Jennifer Cardy (age 9), Susan Claire Maxwell (11), Caroline Hogg (5), and Sarah Harper (10). His general MO was to kidnap, sexually assault, and strangle the girls and then dump their bodies—shoes removed—some distance from the abduction sites. The latter three victims were found in the Midlands area of England, all within a radius of 26 miles; when plotted on a map, the locations formed the shape of a triangle. Because of this, Black's crimes are sometimes called the Midlands Triangle murders.

In 1990 Black attempted to abduct a six-year-old girl in Stow, but he didn't count on a neighbor witnessing a man carrying a piece of cloth toward the girl before she disappeared into a van. The neighbor alerted the girl's mother, and the police intercepted the van and arrested Black. The girl had already been sexually assaulted, but her observant neighbor saved her life and likely the lives of many other little girls as well.

Black pleaded guilty to the sexual assault and abduction of the girl in Stow but refused to confess to any murders. Still, he was sentenced to life imprisonment, and authorities continued to collect evidence in an attempt to bring murder charges. In 1994 Black went on trial for three murders and was convicted, receiving a life sentence for each. He then went on trial for the fourth murder in 2011 and was given another life sentence.

Black died in prison of a heart attack in 2016.

Q: What Australian town considered changing its name because of its connection to serial killers?

A: Snowtown, population less than 500, is about 90 miles north of Adelaide, and during the 1990s it became an unlikely site for the storage of eight bodies, victims of John Bunting, Robert Wagner, James Vlassakis, and Mark Haydon. The Snowtown murders are also called the "bodies-in-barrels murders" because police found the dismembered bodies in drums in an abandoned bank vault in Snowtown. The group is linked to 11 homicides in total.

Bunting is considered the leader of the murder ring, acting out of an extreme hatred for pedophiles, homosexuals, and anyone he considered "weak," which included the intellectually disabled. There were also rumblings of Bunting's Neo-Nazi plan to "purify" Adelaide. Sometimes the quartet accessed the bank accounts of the dead, implying a financial incentive at least some of the time. Their murder and torture methods were as varied as their potential motives and included electric shock, hanging, shooting, and strangulation. Bunting and Wagner cannibalized some victims as well.

After one of the longest trials in Australian history, Bunting received 11 terms of life in prison without parole and Wagner 10 with the same conditions. Vlassakis received four life terms, with a minimum of 26 years, while Haydon was convicted only of helping to dispose of the bodies and was sentenced to 25 years in prison with the possibility of parole after 18.

Ironically, neither the victims nor the killers were from Snowtown, and only one murder even happened there. Nonetheless, the Snowtown murders put this hamlet on the map. Initially Snowtown didn't mind the free press and enjoyed the increased tourism. Still, the lingering stigma led authorities to consider changing the name to Rosetown, though no action has been taken.

Alan Large, an electrician, had big ideas for using the bank as a "gimmick," but the community wasn't interested. "We could have … opened tearooms, sold pies shaped as barrels, spend a night in the vault, that kind of thing," Large told *The Age*, a Melbourne newspaper, in 2011. "But people," he continued with an impressive deadpan, "were just deadly against it."

Q: Who was the University of Texas student whose disappearance led to the downfall of a serial killer and cult leader?

A: Twenty-one-year-old Mark Kilroy was on spring break in Mexico when he disappeared from outside a Matamoros bar in March 1989. By that point Adolfo de Jesus Constanzo and his drug-smuggling crew had already been killing people for a few years for rituals influenced by *palo mayombe* black magic, but the slayings hadn't been a focus for Mexican authorities. The victims tended to be peasants or low-scale drug dealers who weren't really on anyone's radar.

That dynamic changed with pre-med student Kilroy, targeted by Constanzo because of his "superior" brain. Within weeks Constanzo's cult, which had formed because he allegedly possessed psychic powers and performed good luck spells for drug cartels, was firmly within the web of the Mexican police.

When he first began practicing black magic, Constanzo—known as *El Padrino* (the Godfather)—used only animals for sacrifice. Then he moved on to human bones acquired through grave-robbing, and in 1986 he decided he needed live humans. That is when the murders began.

After Kilroy's disappearance, a car carrying four cult members sailed through a roadblock; Constanzo had convinced his followers that his spells gave them a cloak of invisibility, so that may have played a part. They regaled the police with tales of their practices at Rancho Santa Elena. Police raided the ranch the following day and found, in addition to 15 buried, mutilated bodies (including Kilroy's), a cauldron holding a dead black cat, spiders, scorpions, bones, antlers, and a human brain.

Constanzo went on the run, but he was ultimately discovered in a Mexico City apartment with girlfriend Sara Aldrete, a former honors student at Texas Southmost College known as the cult "witch," and five other followers. As part of a death pact, Constanzo ordered Alvaro de Leon Valdez to kill both him and his right-hand man, Martin Quintana Rodriguez, as the police closed in. He did so using a machine gun.

Aldrete, just 24 years old at the time of her arrest, was sentenced to more than 60 years in prison for multiple murders, while de Leon Valdez received a 30-year sentence.

Q: What South Korean killer thanked prosecutors for seeking the death penalty for him?

A: In 2004 Yoo Yeong-cheol confessed to brutally beating 21 people to death with a hammer and then eating some of their livers. He had targeted prostitutes and the wealthy, famously proclaiming to police, "Women shouldn't be sluts, and the rich should know what they've done." He also referred to his victims as "not normal women [who] deserved to be caught by me."

Psychiatrists concluded that Yoo was sane and that his divorce had triggered the murders. Whatever the cause, Yoo's behavior during trial was decidedly bizarre. On one day he jumped over a railing to accost one of the presiding judges, and on another he tried to physically attack a spectator who had cursed him. Before he was permitted to re-enter the courtroom, the judges made him sign a statement swearing he would "not cause any further commotion."

Yoo had dismembered and buried about half of his victims near a Buddhist temple and burned three others. He did express remorse for the killings but added that he would murder a hundred more people if given the chance.

The court didn't give him the chance.

In December 2004 he was convicted of killing 20 people in a 10-month span and was sentenced to death. South Korea hasn't executed anyone since 1997, so despite Yoo's desire "to die before the snow falls," according to his attorney, he still sits on death row.

Chapter 5

LESS FAMOUS SERIAL KILLERS, BUT STILL TRULY AWFUL PEOPLE

Q: What serial killer duo used their victims' clothing to create a "souvenir" quilt?

A: Many serial killers keep "souvenirs" from their victims, but Faye Copeland, who along with her husband Ray began their killing sprees around the ages of 65 and 70, respectively, were extra before being extra was even a thing. Faye actually fashioned a quilt from the clothes worn by their victims.

In his opening statement at Ray Copeland's trial, Missouri Assistant Attorney General Kenny Hulshof quipped, "It is like a book you are going to want to curl up with and read cover to cover." Perhaps this is not the most sensitive way to describe the gory events at the Copeland farm in Mooresville, Missouri, but there's no doubt that this tale is stranger than fiction.

The Copelands were married in the 1940s and had six children. After moving around quite a bit—Ray dabbled in petty crime, so shifting locations was necessary—they settled on a 40-acre farm and began to seek out transients at a mission in Springfield. They offered them room and board and $50 a day in exchange for helping Ray buy cattle.

Ray's side hustle was setting up his employees with checking accounts and having them use bad checks to buy cattle. Before the checks could clear, Ray would drain the accounts and sell the cattle. He had been banned from buying livestock directly because of his own bounced checks.

Eventually Ray got caught and served some jail time, but the real legal problems for the Copelands began when an ex-employee anonymously called a Nebraska crime hotline and dished about his experiences on the farm in August 1989.

Jack McCormick, a self-described "common gutter tramp and drunk," told authorities that he had seen a human skull and leg bone on the Copeland property—and that Ray had tried to kill him. Armed with a search warrant and bloodhounds, a horde of police officers showed up at the farm, but they didn't find any bodies. It wasn't until they expanded their search to other farms where Copeland did odd jobs that they dug up the bodies of three young men at one farm 12 miles south and then, later, two more bodies on other nearby farms.

Paul Jason Cowart, John Freeman, Jimmie Dale Harvey, Wayne Warner, and Dennis Murphy had all been shot in the back of the head at close range with a Marlin .22 caliber bolt-action rifle, which was found in the Copeland residence. All of the men were linked to the Springfield mission from where Copeland had hired farmhands.

The police also discovered Faye's ominous ledger with the names of various farmhands, 12 of whom had an "X" next to their names, including the five victims that had been found. Authorities suspected the Copelands of additional murders, though four of the X-marked men were later found alive.

Faye was convicted on four counts of homicide and one count of manslaughter, while Ray was convicted on five homicide counts. In 1991 the deadly duo became the oldest couple ever sentenced to death in the United States. Ray died of natural causes on death row in prison in 1993.

During her trial, Faye claimed she had suffered years of abuse from Ray. The court—but not the jury—heard testimony from Dr. Marilyn Hutchinson that Faye was, indeed, a "psychologically battered" woman. In 1994 Faye petitioned for a new trial based on the fact that the jury had been prohibited from hearing Hutchinson's testimony. Incidentally, one of the Copeland children testified during the sentencing phase that their father had treated their mother "a lot worse than trash."

In 1999 Faye's death sentence was overturned and her sentence was commuted to five consecutive life terms with no chance of parole. In 2002 Faye suffered a partially paralyzing stroke that left her unable to speak. Missouri Governor Bob Holden allowed her medical parole to a nursing home in her hometown, where she died in 2003.

As for wanting to read the story cover to cover … in the last bizarre twist in this case, you can actually do that in the comic book series *Family Bones* by the Copelands' nephew, Shawn Granger. He spent a summer on the farm with them—and lived to tell the tale.

Q: Who was America's first serial killer family?

A: The Bloody Benders have that distinction, but here's the rub: none of them were actually named Bender.

It is believed that the "Bender" family comprised father John Flickinger ("Pa"), mother Almira Meik ("Ma"), her biological daughter Eliza Griffith ("Kate"), and son John Gebhardt ("John Bender, Jr."). Some say that John was actually Kate's husband, not her brother.

Regardless of their legal names, it is undisputed that this group of four settled into Labette County, Kansas, in the 1870s on two adjacent parcels of land. They ran an inn and store in their one-room home, with an old canvas wagon sheet separating the family quarters from the public area. Travelers journeying across the plains could stop for a rest or top off their supplies of sardines, candy, crackers, horse feed, tobacco, or gunpowder.

Kate was a spiritualist medium who was reportedly quite attractive, so between her beauty and her psychic and healing abilities she drew many men to the inn. But not as many men left as had arrived, which became an issue when Dr. William York, a prominent doctor from Independence, Kansas disappeared and his two also-prominent brothers wouldn't back down in their hunt for him.

The York brothers organized searches that turned up nothing and then approached Kate about using her clairvoyant skills to help find the good doctor. But that night the Benders up and disappeared.

Months later, after a passerby alerted authorities to some starving animals wandering about, town officials broke into the house, which was emitting a "sickening stench." Under a trap door they found a bloody cellar. A dig revealed no bodies, but the group moved on to the always freshly plowed garden plot and discovered York's corpse, barely covered, his throat slit and the back of his skull crushed. Several other similarly injured bodies were found as well.

Authorities believe the Benders killed between 12 and 21 people in all. The theory is that a guest would be seated against the curtain separating public and private spaces, bludgeoned from behind with a hammer while eating, and then dropped through a trap door. There another family member would be waiting to slit the victim's throat and rob him. Two men who refused to sit in the proffered spot by the curtain wound up being verbally abused by Ma Bender—but lived to tell about it.

This theory is supported by two men who refused to sit in the proffered spot by the curtain and wound up being verbally abused by Ma Bender.

One of the victims was a young girl who had gone missing along with her father, whose body was among those found. Based on her remains, authorities didn't believe she died in the same as the manner described above, but records don't specify her cause of death.

It is estimated that the Benders made off with a few thousand dollars, a "good team and wagon," and a pony with saddle for all of that carnage.

No Benders were ever located and positively identified, let alone brought to justice, and nothing is left of the old homestead. The only thing that remains, at a rest stop at the junction of US Routes 400 and 169 north of Cherrydale, is a historical marker telling the grisly tale of the Bloody Benders.

The documentary series *Evil Kin* tells the Bloody Benders' story in Season 2, Episode 2.

Q: What was the final resting place of Texas bootlegger Joe Ball's victims?

A: They ended up in an alligator pit in back of Ball's roadhouse in Elmendorf, Texas.

In the late 1930s, the media coined the term "Murder Farm" to describe Ball's tavern—behind which, it turned out, he fed the body parts of women he had killed to his five full-grown alligators. Ball even made alligator feeding time into a show to entertain customers.

Unfortunately for Ball, when hostess Hazel Brown went missing, that was one too many women connected with him or his tavern to have disappeared. Along with four other former hostesses, the list included his second wife, Nell. Police showed up with questions about Brown, and after calmly fielding them he bid the officers good-bye and shot himself through the heart.

After Ball's suicide, handyman Clifford Wheeler told authorities that he had seen Ball kill Brown with a hatchet and dissect her body. Then he had helped bury her.

Another man also came forward to recount his experience in 1932, when he had surprised Ball behind the tavern as he was dragging a woman's body to the alligator pit. The anonymous man left town after Ball threatened him and his family if he were to tell anyone what he had seen. He only returned to tell the police his story after he heard of Ball's death.

Where Ball's life went wrong is unclear, as he came into the world as the son of one of the founding members of his small town in south

Texas. He was the first man from Elmendorf to enlist in World War I. Sometime after that, however, things went terribly awry.

Ball's story became the inspiration for Tobe Hooper's 1976 film *Eaten Alive*, about the owner of a seedy Texas motel who feeds human victims to an alligator in the nearby swamp.

In 1963 Ball's third wife—by then Mrs. Herbert Stiles—called Ball "a pretty good man" and said the whole thing about his feeding body parts to alligators was untrue. "Legend is strong," she said, and noted that she had lost an arm in a car accident but people would still gossip and say, "Joe put her in with the alligators."

Q: What plot did Lawrence Bittaker and Roy Norris hatch while serving time together?

A: In prison at the California Men's Colony in San Luis Obispo for different crimes, Bittaker and Norris became fast friends in 1978 over a shared interest in abducting, raping, and killing teenage girls—one for each age, 13 to 19—and memorializing the acts on film and audio recordings.

Bittaker got out of prison first and started getting things ready for Norris' release seven months later, including preparation of the Murder Mack, the 1979 silver GMC van the two would use in their crimes. Norris had only been free for nine days when they nabbed 16-year-old Lucinda Schaeffer on June 24, 1979. Then 18-year-old Andrea Joy Hall disappeared, followed by 13-year-old Jacqueline Leah Lamp and 15-year-old Jackie Doris Gilliam—whose body was eventually found with an ice pick still in her ear cavity. The pair also used a sledgehammer and pliers to torture and kill their young victims, leading to the nickname Toolbox Killers.

On November 1, police found the terribly bruised and battered body of Shirley Linett Ledford. The 16-year-old had suffered "sadistic and barbaric abuse," including mutilation of her breasts and face. She had been strangled with a coat hanger. The victims had often been brutally tortured and sexually assaulted for hours or days before they died.

That month Norris bragged about the murders to a former prison friend, who told authorities. Realizing that the stories matched up with the murder of Ledford as well as several unsolved rapes and attempted abductions, police showed photos of the pair to one victim who had described a van similar to the Murder Mack. She positively identified Norris and Bittaker as her attackers.

Police watched Norris until they caught him selling marijuana a few days later and arrested him; they also arrested Bittaker, also in possession of drugs, for rape and abduction. The victim couldn't pick the men out of a lineup, but since having drugs violated their parole conditions, they remained in custody.

Norris gradually spilled everything about their murders to police and led them to two graves in San Dimas Canyon in the San Gabriel Mountains. Upon finding 500 candid shots of young women and girls and an audio recording of Ledford's death in the murder van, police suspected the duo of an additional 30 or 40 murders. After Bittaker's trial, one juror admitted she had nightmares because of Ledford's piercing screams and pleas for her life.

Norris flipped on Bittaker and received a sentence of 45 years to life, while Bittaker tried to pin it all on Norris. But the jury found Bittaker guilty and took only an hour and a half to give him the death penalty. He is still on death row at San Quentin State Prison in California.

Postscript: From their respective prisons, Norris and Bittaker resumed their friendship as pen pals. Their correspondence occasionally shows up for sale on murderabilia sites.

Q: Who was the Coast to Coast serial killer?

A: Tommy Lynn Sells was thought to be responsible for as many as 70 deaths but was convicted of just two. He traveled the country from 1979 to 1999, indiscriminately raping and murdering men, women, and children—and it would be a child who led to his capture.

On December 31, 1999, Sells broke into the Harris home near Del Rio, Texas and attacked 13-year-old Kaylene Harris and 10-year-old Krystal Surles. The younger girl saw Sells slash her friend's throat and played dead, all the while gathering enough of a mental image of the killer to relay to police. Her description formed the basis of a sketch that enabled authorities to identify and arrest him two days later at his home.

And then Sells started talking.

After a childhood of abandonment by his single mother, sexual abuse from a male adult, and early drug and alcohol abuse, Sells became a drifter, stealing or doing odd jobs for money. He claimed he committed his first murder at age 16, when he broke into a house and killed a man who was performing oral sex on a boy; authorities have never corroborated his story.

Over his 20 years of murdering, if Sells didn't actually target single mothers and their children, it sure was a heckuva coincidence as many of his victims fit that profile.

One of the most disturbing victim tales, though, is that of the Dardeen family in Illinois. Keith Dardeen had picked up the hitchhiking Sells and taken him home to give him a hot meal. As thanks, Sells shot Dardeen and cut off his penis. He then killed Dardeen's three-year-old son by cracking his skull with a hammer and tried to rape Dardeen's pregnant wife, Elaine, who went into labor. Sells killed both mother and newborn by beating them with a baseball bat and placed the murder weapon inside Elaine's vagina.

Sells confessed to the Dardeen murders, though some remain skeptical of his admission and he was never tried for the Illinois crimes.

Instead, on September 18, 2000, he was sentenced to death by a Texas jury for the murder of Kaylene Harris. He later also pleaded guilty in the strangling death of nine-year-old Mary Bea Perez in San Antonio.

Sells died by lethal injection in 2014 at the Texas State Penitentiary.

Q: What canine evidence helped bring the Trash Bag Killer to justice?

A: Patrick Kearney targeted boys and young homosexual men for more than a decade before he was apprehended in 1977 after hairs from his two poodles were found on the body of his final victim, 17-year-old John Otis LaMay. Kearney confessed to 38 murders, though prosecutors were only able to verify and charge him with 21 of them.

Authorities didn't even begin linking the murders until April 1975, with the discovery of the naked body of 21-year-old Albert Rivera off Highway 74 near San Juan Capistrano, California. Shot in the head with a .22 caliber pistol, he had been wrapped in nylon and filament tape and shoved into a black plastic trash bag. This would prove to be Kearney's usual murder and disposal method.

Nearly two years would pass before the discovery of LaMay's body—minus his head, feet, and hands—off Highway 71 in Riverside County in March 1977. The last LaMay's mother had heard from him, he had said he was going to see his friend "Dave." Authorities were able to learn from another of LaMay's friends that Dave was David Hill; he was even able to give them the address in Redondo Beach.

Police showed up at the house, which was owned by Kearney, and questioned its occupants. Hill admitted to sexual activity with LaMay, but authorities weren't able to link Kearney to any crimes until they obtained a search warrant. Then they found a blood-stained hacksaw, human blood in the shower matching LaMay's blood type, and pubic hair, carpet fibers, and the dog hair—all of which matched those found on LaMay.

Aware that authorities were on to them, Kearney and Hill went on the run, the former leaving lengthy instructions for his grandmother to sell his house and other possessions and pay off his debts—lest he, ahem, be thrown in jail. The pair fled to Mexico but returned to turn themselves in at the urging of family.

"That's us," they said, after walking into the Riverside County Sheriff's office and pointing at a wanted poster on the wall.

Hill was soon released from custody, as police couldn't definitely link him to the murders, but Kearney was eventually convicted of 21 murders and is serving life in prison without parole.

Q: Who was the first American convicted of using insulin as a murder weapon?

A: William Dale Archerd, also known as James Lynn Arden, was found guilty on three counts of murder in California in 1968 after injecting victims with insulin overdoses that brought about lethal hypoglycemia. Among his victims were two of his seven wives and a 15-year-old nephew; he was also suspected in the deaths of another former wife and two male friends.

Archerd was sentenced to death, but that was commuted to life imprisonment when the California Supreme Court struck down the death penalty statute. He died of natural causes in 1977.

Archerd's experience with insulin began when he worked as an attendant at the Camarillo State Mental Hospital, which used insulin shock therapies on patients. He was placed on probation for two counts of felony morphine possession in 1950 and served time in prison; he said he changed his name to James Lynn Arden upon his release.

Interesting side note: When it ran the story of Archerd's conviction, the Honolulu Star-Bulletin openly speculated whether a William Dale Archerd suspected of transporting a bomb on a plane from Los Angeles to Honolulu in 1961 was the same person as the man just convicted of murder.

The available evidence suggested a connection, as the physical descriptions matched and potential bomber Archerd had taken out life insurance policies naming twin sons as beneficiaries. The convicted killer Archerd did have twin sons—and insurance money was considered a possible motive in his insulin-related killings, though he only collected about $10,000.

Q: What serial killer did James Woods portray in the film *Killer: A Journal of Murder*?

A: Woods played Carl Panzram, who besides being a murderer was also an admitted rapist, arsonist, and thief. The 1996 film was inspired by a 1970 book by Thomas E. Gaddis and James O. Long, which was based on Panzram's own writings, penned surreptitiously while he was incarcerated—prisoners weren't permitted to have writing materials.

A kindly guard named Henry Lesser facilitated Panzram's writing, though, and his efforts at making them known—including correspondence with H.L. Mencken, psychiatrist Karl Menninger, and criminologist Sheldon Glueck—ultimately resulted in the publication of this riveting volume 40 years after Panzram's execution. Menninger published his own work on Panzram—*Man Against Himself*—under the pseudonym John Smith, identifying Panzram only by his prison number. Aside from the gruesome details of his life and crimes, Panzram's writings provide fascinating insight into the criminal justice system and prison reform.

Panzram was born on a Minnesota farm in 1891, and his life started to go off track early on. In his own words, "I have been a human animal ever since I was born." Before he reached teenhood, Panzram had encounters with the juvenile court for drunkenness and stealing. His two-year stint in the Minnesota State Training School beginning in 1903 certainly did more harm than good. He was regularly beaten in the "paint shop"—so named "because there they used to paint our bodies black and blue." The school taught him mainly "about man's inhumanity to man." Things only went downhill from there.

By his own estimate, Panzram committed 21 murders of men and young boys, several arsons, hundreds of burglaries and robberies, and the sodomy of a thousand people. Among his claims are that he robbed the New Haven, Connecticut, home of Chief Justice William Howard Taft and that he shot six men and fed their bodies to crocodiles in Africa. Panzram makes it clear that he isn't "in the least bit sorry" for his actions, though he did point out that he was sorry for the few times he mistreated animals—and also "sorry that I am unable to murder the whole damned human race."

The descriptions of his crimes are often graphic but always detached and unemotional. When writing about his rape and murder of an 11- or 12-year-old boy in Portuguese Angola, Panzram said that the boy's "brains were coming out of his ears." A 10-year-old Philadelphia boy Panzram said he had killed in 1922 was indeed found with his "brains smashed in by stone," making his claims disturbingly believable.

When Panzram got pinched in Baltimore for stealing jewelry in Washington, DC, his extensive criminal record meant a sentence of 25 years to life. Upon arrival at Fort Leavenworth Penitentiary in Kansas, Inmate #31614 informed the warden that he didn't play well with others, so he was placed in solitary confinement. Still, that didn't contain Panzram's murderous ways; he beat a prison employee to death with an iron bar. For that crime, he was sentenced to death and was hanged in 1930.

Lesser, the keeper of Panzram's autobiographical writings, spoke to a criminal justice class at San Diego State University in 1979. Thereafter he donated the "Carl Panzram papers" to the school, which has digitized many of them and made them available online.

Q: Who was the Eyeball Killer?

A: Charles Albright, the Dallas serial killer known for removing his victims' eyes, lived a double life as a murderer of prostitutes and a carpenter his neighbors called "the gentlest man" they knew.

Albright may have been gentle, but he had certainly had extensive experience in the criminal justice system by the time his 1991 murder trial came around. He was still on 10 years' probation for a 1985 conviction of aggravated sexual assault of a child. He had also served two years for stealing equipment from a lumberyard, and just a month before his arrest on murder charges he had pleaded guilty to stealing $190 worth of baseball cards from Walmart.

The work of some truly crack detectives probably saved a lot of women's lives in Dallas, as Albright's rampage lasted just three months. Still, in that short time he claimed three victims, all of whom he had sex with before shooting them in the head (sometimes more than once), removing their eyeballs, and taking them from the scene.

The 57-year-old Albright was arrested when detectives zeroed in on him as a suspect and a woman Albright had attempted to murder identified him through photos. Then the forensic team moved in and linked a blue blanket in Albright's pickup with fibers found on two of the victims. Moreover, hair from a victim was on the blanket, and Albright's hair was found on one victim.

Albright was convicted of the murders and sentenced to life in prison with no chance of parole.

Q: What two killers appeared on TV game shows during their murder sprees?

A: On the US side of the pond, Rodney Alcala is known as the Dating Game Killer because he was a contestant on that matchmaking show, while Welsh serial killer John Cooper is called the Bullseye Killer for his appearance on the British game show Bullseye. Both were done in by DNA many years after their crimes. Oddly enough, both were 66 years old at the time of their convictions, which were handed down about a year apart.

In 2010 Alcala was convicted on five murder counts, including the 1979 death of 12-year-old Robin Samsoe. The four other victims were women ages 18 to 32, killed between 1977 and 1979. Two previous convictions for the Samsoe murder had been overturned on appeal, explaining the long lag from crime to conviction. Alcala has also been linked with at least six other murders, and he was brutal. He raped one victim with a claw hammer and strangled women to the point of their passing out, only to resuscitate them so he could start the terror all over again.

Alcala had already served time for rape when he was a contestant on *The Dating Game* and won a date with the bachelorette—who made an excellent decision to refuse the offer because she thought he was creepy.

When a police sketch of the Samsoe perpetrator circulated, Alcala's parole officer identified him. A subsequent search of his storage locker revealed two pairs of earrings that he had kept as trophies. Alcala, who represented himself in his 2010 trial and even cross-examined "the defendant" using two different voices, tried to argue that the earrings were his and that he wore them during his game show appearance. But a fellow contestant refuted that testimony, saying that earrings as fashion accessories for men weren't yet common in 1978 and he would have remembered had Alcala worn them.

Alcala lured victims by pretending to be a professional photographer. In fact, in that storage locker authorities found hundreds of photographs of women and girls, the vast majority too sexually explicit to be released to the public for identification.

Across the pond, in 2011 Cooper received four life sentences with no possibility of parole for the 1985 murders of Richard and Helen Thomas and the 1989 murders of Peter and Gwenda Dixon in Pembrokeshire. Robbing his victims was paramount for Cooper, and footage from Cooper's 1989 appearance on the telly was what actually helped identify him.

Like Alcala, Cooper had been on the police radar for quite some time before evidence emerged linking him to murder. A convicted rapist, armed robber, and burglar, Cooper used a sawed-off shotgun as his weapon of choice. That eventually helped lead to his arrest when, about a decade after the crime, blood found under paint on the gun was identified as belonging to one of his victims. Shorts recovered at his home also linked him to the murders through DNA.

Q: Who was the Scorecard Killer who kept a coded list of his murders?

A: On May 14, 1983, Randy Kraft was pulled over by California Highway Patrol officers for driving erratically. At most, they probably thought he was under the influence of alcohol or drugs. They couldn't have expected to find a dead body in the passenger seat.

Hand it to Kraft, he did try to steer officers away by getting out of his car and approaching their vehicle instead of waiting for them to come to him. Needless to say, the officers caught on quickly, found the lifeless body of 25-year-old Marine Terry Gambrel, and arrested Kraft on the spot.

Subsequent searches yielded especially solid evidence against Kraft, including photographs of three missing men and a large collection of notes, handwritten in some kind of code, which authorities later deciphered to be a rundown of the details on all of Kraft's murders. A prosecutor referred to these as a kind of "scorecard," giving Kraft his nickname.

On the forensic side, investigators matched fibers from a rug in Kraft's garage with those found on the body of one of his victims. Police also found objects that had gone missing from the scenes of unsolved murders in Michigan and Oregon and pieced together that Kraft had visited those areas during the times of the crimes.

As it turned out, Kraft had been raping, murdering, mutilating, and dismembering mostly homosexual males for at least the previous 10 years. In 1989 he was convicted on 16 counts of murder and sentenced to die. On death row at California's San Quentin State Prison, he made friends with fellow serial killers Douglas Clark, Lawrence Bittaker, and William Bonin, who was executed in 1996.

Q: Who did Tony Costa claim killed some of his victims?

A: Costa killed four to eight women in the late 1960s, and his book *Resurrection* details the murders of two of them—by his friend "Carl." He also claims that "Carl" dismembered the bodies of two other victims after they died of drug overdoses.

Costa's murders spanned three states (California, Massachusetts, and New York), and his killing methods varied. His disturbing behavior started in his teens, when he was caught trying to drag a teenage girl from her bed in Somerville, Massachusetts. A few days earlier he had been caught standing over her as she slept. He was given a one-year suspended sentence and three years' probation in 1962.

In June 1966 he brought two girls to the house he shared with his wife, saying he was going to take them to California—but the girls were never seen again. Costa was also linked to the 1968 disappearance of Barbara Spaulding, who also was never found.

That same year, Costa killed Sydney Monzon, Susan Perry, and Christine Gallant. He raped Monzon after her death and removed her heart.

In 1969 Patricia Walsh and Mary Anne Wysocki had the great misfortune of happening across Costa, and they became his victims as well. Just as he had done with Monzon, Costa raped their corpses and removed their hearts.

Costa was convicted on four murder charges in 1970 and sentenced to life imprisonment, but he only served four years before he hanged himself in his cell in Walpole, Massachusetts.

Q: What city's Italian population was targeted by a murder ring in the 1930s?

A: With its lively open-air Italian market lined with pasta, cheese, and cured meats, South Philadelphia has long been known as the home of the city's Italian immigrant population. Just after the Great Depression, however, the zone was struggling to stay afloat financially. That created the perfect atmosphere for the murder-for-hire scheme cooked up by some cousins from the neighborhood, who also operated a branch out of North Philly for good measure.

Spaghetti salesman Herman Petrillo and his cousin Paul got together with Morris Bolder and ex-con Cesare "Jumbo" Valente to arrive at one of the deadliest insurance scams in history. Along with two primary women accomplices, Rose Carina and Maria Carina Favato, and a whole lot of Old Country witchcraft, the group endeavored to match widows with new husbands, many of whom were Italian immigrants whose lives would be insured. The husband would have an "accident" and the policies would pay out—double in the case of accidental death. The new widows and the schemers would each get a cut of the proceeds.

Because many of the victims were poisoned, the murderers became known as the Arsenic Gang once the full story became known. Others were drowned or killed in fake car accidents, but it was the arsenic that began to do in the murder ring when so many Italian immigrants wound up dead with high levels of the poison in their bodies.

The real blow came when Herman Petrillo, already suspected of counterfeiting, offered George Myers $500 to kill Ferdinand Alfonsi by hitting him with a lead pipe and arranging it took as if he had been run over by a car. Myers provided the information to the government.

Alfonsi ended up dying of arsenic poisoning, and Herman Petrillo and his wife Stella were charged with murder. Several bodies were exhumed and re-examined, and when it was all sorted, law enforcement confirmed 27 deaths and estimated that between 50 and 100 may have died at the hands of the murder ring. Once he was facing the death penalty, Herman Petrillo "squealed his head off," as did Carina Favato in an attempt to save her life.

Many of the wives were charged with crimes as well, but most flipped for the state. The Petrillos received death sentences and were executed in 1941, while others received life in prison.

In an ironic twist, the Prudential Life Insurance Company tried to get out of paying on Paul Petrillo's $5,000 life insurance policy after his execution, arguing that it would be "against public policy" to do so. A Philadelphia federal judge didn't buy it.

Q: Who were the Lonely Hearts Killers?

A: In the late 1940s Raymond Martinez Fernandez and Martha Beck took out personal ads to lure women, only to then steal their money and kill them.

The *New York Daily News* called the couple Mr. and Mrs. Bluebeard, describing Fernandez as "a swarthy, stoop-shouldered, balding manual laborer with a gold front tooth" and Beck as "a 200-pound, gap-toothed nurse."

Fernandez was the mastermind behind the scheme, which went like this: Upon paying a matrimonial agency $2 for contact information from a list of "lonely hearts," he would write to the women, supposedly looking for love. Then he would travel to meet them, seduce them, steal their money, and do away with them.

After wooing and stealing from one Manhattan widow, Fernandez collected insurance money from another women killed in a "train accident" and traveled to Florida to meet Beck, who was also on the lonely hearts list. Beck followed Fernandez back to New York, and since he didn't want her two toddlers around, she left them at the Salvation Army. The pair decided to continue his scheme together, with Beck posing as his sister.

They traveled the country from Arkansas to Vermont and then back to New York, where the pair killed Janet Fay of Albany and buried her at their house in Queens, pouring concrete over her body. Fernandez then set his sights on Delphine Downing in Grand Rapids, Michigan. After three days of seduction, Downing started transferring her money to Fernandez, but she became suspicious when he showed up with a new $104 toupee.

Beck gave Downing sleeping pills, and as she slept Fernandez wrapped his gun in blankets and shot her. The pair buried Downing in her own basement and covered her with concrete. Over the next few days Downing's two-year-old daughter wouldn't stop crying for her mommy, so the killers drowned and buried her, too.

Then one night, upon returning from a movie the couple was met at the door by detectives investigating Downing's disappearance. The police pushed past them and discovered the newly poured concrete, and the Lonely Hearts game was over. Among Fernandez's belongings was a list of 132 names, with 14 checked off. While the number of victims may have been as high as 17, only four murders were ever officially linked to the pair.

As for the murderous couple, the two professed their love for one another in written statements before their deaths. They had not been allowed any contact during the 19 months they waited on death row.

Both were executed for their crimes in 1951 at New York's Sing Sing Prison. They died six minutes apart, Fernandez first.

Q: What name was given to the San Francisco killings by the Death Angels in the 1970s?

A: They were known as the Zebra Murders. The Death Angels were a group of Muslim men—a splinter group of the Fruit of Islam, the security branch of the Nation of Islam—who targeted whites, especially "blue-eyed devils." In the span of less than six months in 1973–1974 the sect killed 15 people and injured another seven—including Art Agnos, who would become the city's mayor in the late 1980s. In addition to murder, the group raped at least two women.

The Zebra name didn't come from the black/white aspect of the case, but because the radio channel used by the police to communicate about the case was "Z for Zebra."

Complicating law enforcement's handling of the crimes was the general racial tension in the city and in the police department itself then. Years later, Prentice Earl Sanders, one of two black homicide inspectors at the time, wrote about the case in his memoir, *The Zebra Murders: A Season of Killing, Racial Madness, and Civil Rights*. Sanders, who later became San Francisco's first black police chief, described a department severely ill-equipped to handle the case. He blamed racism for keeping "the department so white we didn't have enough black officers to infiltrate a group like the one we were after."

Also coming under heavy criticism were the investigation techniques, which largely consisted of racial profiling—i.e, repeatedly stopping black men on the street. Some blacks were stopped so many times that the city began doling out special identification cards they could flash to officers to stop further useless interrogations. The National

Association for the Advancement of Colored People (NAACP) filed a federal lawsuit to stop the practice as unconstitutional and won.

The police caught a lucky break when 28-year-old Anthony Harris came forward, confessed, and gave the names of eight other Death Angels killers. On May 1, 1974, more than 100 officers conducted several separate raids to round up the suspects. Though four were let go because no solid evidence linked them to crimes, another four were tried and convicted for the killings. Jessie Lee Cooks, J.C.X. Simon, Larry Green, and Manuel Moore all received life sentences.

Simon died in prison in 2015. The other three remain in prison with the possibility of parole.

Q: What child killer influenced the Nebraska Supreme Court to rule the electric chair "cruel and unusual"?

A: John Joubert's skin was severely burned in several places during his 1996 execution by electric chair, and he also received a "brain blister" on top of his head. His injuries eventually helped push a 2008 Nebraska Supreme Court decision that electrocution is "cruel and unusual punishment." The state switched to lethal injection thereafter.

Joubert was just 20 years old when he was arrested for the murders of 13-year-old Danny Joe Eberle and 12-year-old Christopher Walden. On September 18, 1983, Eberle disappeared on his newspaper route in Bellevue, Nebraska. His body—clad only in underwear, gagged with tape, bound at the wrist and ankles, and brutally stabbed—was discovered days later. In addition to nine stab wounds, Eberle had sustained human bite marks. A witness reported seeing a tan car in the area.

Walden disappeared on December 2 not far from where Eberle's body had been found, and the similarities between the two cases were obvious, especially the knife wounds. In Walden's case, his head was nearly severed by a slash across his throat. This time witnesses had seen the boy get into a tan sedan.

About a month later, day care center owner Barbara Weaver, surely always on the lookout for "stranger danger," noticed a white car lurking around her building. She jotted down the license plate and notified police, who traced it to a local dealership. Joubert had taken his tan car in for repair and gotten the white loaner, which led authorities directly to his barracks at Offut Air Force Base. A search there turned up a hunting knife and rope matching what had been used to tie up Eberle.

Joubert confessed, admitting he had harbored sexually violent fantasies since he was a young boy. He was also eventually convicted for the murder of 11-year-old Richard Stetson in Maine, where he was given a superfluous life sentence.

After a last meal of pizza, salad with Catalina dressing, strawberry cheesecake, and black coffee, Joubert was executed on July 17, 1996. He was 33 years old.

Q: What serial killer's construction company once employed Robin Gecht, leader of the Chicago Rippers?

A: Gecht had worked for John Wayne Gacy's company at one time. How's that for a creepy construction crew?

Gecht was considered the ringleader of a satanic group that abducted, raped, murdered, and mutilated young women in Chicago in the early 1980s.

After his arrest in 1982, police found evidence of a "satanic chapel" at Gecht's apartment: a candlelit attic featuring an altar draped in a red cloth and walls decorated with black and red crosses. Here the Ripper Crew would read passages from the Satanic Bible before torturing their victims with various objects (including knives and ice picks), gang raping them, and then severing one or both of their breasts with a wire garrote. Each participant would eat some of the breast as "communion," and then Gecht would masturbate into the breast before storing it in a trophy box. Accomplice Tom Kokoraleis claimed the box had contained at least 15 breasts at one time.

The other members of the cult were Tom's brother Andrew and Edward Spreitzer. In all, the group is believed to be responsible for the deaths or disappearances of 18 women in an 18-month span.

Their spree ended after they thought they had disposed of the dead body of 20-year-old Beverly Washington near some railroad tracks—but she was still alive and was able to tell her tale. Authorities didn't yet have enough evidence to nail the murder ring, but then they discovered that the four men had rented adjoining rooms at Villa

Park's Rip Van Winkle Motel some time back. The motel was near where some of the Chicago Rippers' victims were found.

The trail led first to Tom Kokoraleis; he turned on his fellow cult members, leading to further arrests. Tom ended up receiving a life sentence for murder and related felonies, but on appeal he got a new trial and a reduced 70-year sentence for pleading guilty. He was scheduled to be released in September 2017 for good behavior, but because he didn't have an approved place to live after getting out, his release was pushed back until September 2020.

His brother Andrew received the stiffest penalty possible and died by lethal injection in 1999—the last inmate to be executed before Illinois put a moratorium on the death penalty. Spreitzer was also sentenced to death but saw his penalty commuted to life in prison in 2003.

As for Gecht? Well, he has yet to be tried for murder. Instead he received a 120-year sentence for rape, attempted murder, and aggravated battery—and is eligible for parole in 2022.

Q: What serial rapist and murderer recruited his own teenage son to help commit crimes?

A: Joseph Kallinger, the Shoemaker, even killed one of his own sons—apparently just for the thrill of it.

Kallinger had survived a difficult upbringing to be sure, raised by adoptive parents who brutally beat him and demonized anything sexual; they even tried to convince young Joe that he had been castrated during a hernia operation. They appeared to want a child simply for his contributions to the family shoemaking business, and Kallinger did indeed become a shoemaker—thus his nickname.

Over 18 months between 1973 and January 1975, Kallinger and his teenage son Michael broke into the homes of families in Pennsylvania, Maryland, and New Jersey to rob them. Joe often sexually assaulted the female victims as well. He killed one woman for refusing to bite off the penis of a male victim in the house.

The pair drowned Joseph, Jr.—Joe's son and Michael's brother—at a demolition site. Joe later said that Michael hated his brother "because Joey was a homosexual."

The killings stopped after Joe left behind a bloody shirt at one of the crime scenes, leading police to him.

Michael was judged by New Jersey courts to be "salvageable," which meant he was placed on probation until the age of 25. He claimed his father tortured him and has since changed his name—and hopefully his life, for the better.

For his part, Joe tried to use an insanity plea, but it was rejected three times. He was eventually convicted on multiple felony counts. At one of his trials, the judge commented at sentencing, "You are an evil man, Mr. Kallinger, utterly vile and depraved."

Joe spent some time at Pennsylvania's Fairview State Hospital for the Criminally Insane and was on suicide watch for the last five years of his life after harming himself by swallowing foreign objects such as paper clips and his own glasses, and tying rubber bands around his wrists to cut off blood circulation. He died of natural causes in 1996.

Q: Who was the Casanova Killer?

A: Paul John "PJ" Knowles, dubbed the Casanova Killer for his good looks and charm, was described as a "dreamboat" by British journalist Sandy Fawkes. She shared a romantic evening with Knowles before they traveled to Miami together to see friends—and she lived to tell about it.

"He was tall, fair, and handsome, with the immaculate manner of the comfortably rich American"—that's how the *London Daily Express* writer described the man she had met just two weeks before he was arrested in 1974 for multiple murders. Looks were decidedly deceiving, however, as Knowles also reportedly strived to be the greatest mass murderer in modern history.

True to his nickname, Knowles began his crime binge with the promise of cross-country love. He had been in prison in Florida for a burglary conviction when he began corresponding with a San Francisco woman named Angela Covic. She hooked Knowles up with attorney Sheldon Yavitz, who got Knowles released on parole in 1974 on the condition that he get a job in San Francisco. Knowles did make his way out there, but Covic, disturbed by Knowles' "aura of fear" and a warning from a psychic who told her a dangerous man was coming into her life, sent him packing on a plane back to Jacksonville. Knowles claimed that he had killed three people before leaving California, though that has never been proven.

Back in Florida, Knowles got into a bar fight and was sent back to jail, but he escaped and that same night claimed the first East Coast victim, 65-year-old Alice Curtis. Knowles broke into her home, gagged and bound her, and went about stealing whatever he could grab. Curtis died by choking on her dentures.

On November 17, 1974, Trooper Charles Eugene Campbell pulled Knowles over because he recognized the car as stolen, but Knowles was ready for the encounter. He took Campbell's cruiser, with the officer as a hostage. Then, to be even more inconspicuous, he stole another car and took that owner as hostage, too. He quickly realized that traveling with two hostages wasn't a great idea, so he took both men into the woods in Georgia, tied to them to trees, and shot each of them in the head.

Meanwhile, police had set up roadblocks. Knowles crashed through one of them and plowed into a tree, leading to a foot chase. He might have gotten away if it hadn't been for a deer hunter he happened upon and asked for help. The hunter didn't help; instead he used his own gun to escort Knowles to the police.

By the time he was arrested, the 28-year-old Knowles had killed, by his own estimate, 35 people in a four-month span. His crimes were as random as they were heinous—information that may or may not have been verified by Knowles' taped diary, which was released to authorities but never made public. The victims included elderly women, young girls, and men, and besides murder he added rape and robbery. He also stole a few cars along the way. Most of his victims were strangled, though some were shot.

Knowles never saw a trial, however. A month after his arrest, he was traveling with Sheriff Earl Lee and Georgia Bureau of Investigation Agent Ronnie Angel to show them where he had dumped the gun used to shoot Campbell. When he tried to wrestle away the sheriff's gun, Agent Angel shot him.

Attorney Yavitz continued to defend his client even after his death. He told the media that Knowles must have been set up for his final blaze of glory, since he had to have been in arm or leg shackles, or both.

Q: Why did Leonard Lake and Charles Ng keep sex slaves as part of Operation Miranda?

A: This unlikely pair believed the world would soon be ravaged by nuclear war and that, once the mushroom clouds dissipated, it was up to them to rebuild the human species with sex slaves they kept in a Northern California bomb shelter.

Their Operation Miranda was named for the main character in John Fowles' novel *The Collector*, which tells the tale of a woman who is kidnapped and held captive by a psychopath.

Between 1983 and 1985, in addition to individual victims, Lake and Ng kidnapped at least two families that each included a man, a woman, and a child. Sometimes they would make the men and children watch their brutal torture and sexual assaults of the women. Then they would keep the women alive in a specially constructed cinder-block bunker so long as they didn't get bored with them.

Their crimes became known after Ng was seen shoplifting on June 2, 1985. While Ng seemed to have vanished, a comb of the parking lot revealed Lake sitting in his car with a gun. He produced a fake ID, and that eventually led to a search of Lake's cabin of horrors. Police found 40 or so pounds of crushed and burnt bones, Ng's diaries, and victim IDs—all of which led investigators to conclude that there had been at least 25 victims. And in case there was any doubt as to the brutality of the crimes, Lake and Ng had videotaped their assaults; two such records were found on the property.

Ng managed to escape to Canada but was picked up there for shoplifting. After he served time up north, our good neighbors shipped him back to California despite his argument that the Golden State had the death penalty, whereas Canada did not.

In fact, Ng was convicted and sentenced to death in one of the longest and most expensive trials in California history. It took six years and $20 million to finally obtain Ng's conviction in 1999, and he still sits on death row today.

Lake, on the other hand, didn't even last a full day in custody. As he awaited questioning, he casually ripped out two pills sewn inside his shirt collar and swallowed them with a glass of water. They were cyanide, and he died four days later.

Q: What makes brothers Danny and Larry Ranes unique among related killers?

A: The Ranes brothers of Kalamazoo, Michigan are both serial killers, but they committed all of their murders separately, each without any knowledge that the other was also killing people.

Perhaps for those who knew the brothers personally this isn't surprising, as the two apparently enjoyed a lifelong competition with one another, starting from when their alcoholic, abusive father would make them brawl over quarters on the floor. At one point, the brothers even competed for the affections of the same woman.

For whatever it's worth, Larry killed first. When he was just 19 years old, he went on a cross-country killing "adventure"—hitchhiking, robbing, and murdering at least five men along the way. Gary Smock's body was found in May 1964, and when police showed up at Larry's door he was wearing the dead man's watch and shoes. From there he confessed that he had been busier than just committing Smock's murder. Three victims were gas station attendants, a fact he later tried to use to explain why he killed: His abusive father had been a gas station attendant, the argument went—but the jury didn't buy it.

Larry was sentenced to life in prison and legally changed his name to Monk Steppenwolf, after the Herman Hesse character.

Danny, on the other hand, was convicted of raping and killing women, sometimes with an accomplice, 15-year-old Brent Koster, who flipped on his older murder-mate under the promise of a reduced sentence. Danny maintained his innocence but is also serving a life sentence.

If you think you've heard this story but not the name "Ranes," you might have read the book *Luke Karamazov* by Conrad Hilberry, in which he tells the true story of the Ranes brothers but calls them Ralph and Tommy Searl. "Luke Karamazov" was Hilberry's choice to replace Larry Ranes' new moniker of "Monk Steppenwolf."

Q: What serial killer's discussions about the Marquis de Sade led to his arrest?

A: When Melvin David Rees, known as Dave, waxed poetic about the sadistic ideas of the French nobleman, his friend Glenn Moser began to wonder just how seriously Rees was taking their philosophical questions. Then came a series of unexplained murders in the greater Washington, DC, area in the late 1950s. Moser knew it was time to inform authorities, especially after a composite sketch by a surviving victim looked an awful lot like the friend with whom he had grown up and attended the University of Maryland.

On June 26, 1957, Margaret Harold, age 36, was with her boyfriend, Army Sgt. Roy D. Hudson, when Rees accosted them with a .38 caliber gun. Hudson was tied to a tree, but he managed to escape and go for help. By the time he got back, though, Harold was dead and had been sexually assaulted.

Then on January 11, 1959, a car carrying a family from Apple Grove, Virginia was run off the road. Two months later authorities found the bodies of Carroll Jackson, 29, and one-year-old Janet near Fredericksburg, Virginia. Rees had tied up Carroll and shot him with a .38 caliber pistol and then placed the still-living Janet beneath him in a ditch; the toddler suffocated to death under the weight of her father. The bodies of Carroll's wife, Mildred, 27, and daughter Susan Ann, five, were discovered in March some 80 miles away.

Once police zeroed in on Rees with Moser's help, they found a .38 gun with human blood on the trigger at his family's home in Hyattsville,

Maryland. There was also a "diary of sorts" detailing the Jackson family killing and including a newspaper photo of Mildred and Susan Ann.

"Caught on a lonely road … Drove to select area and killed husband and baby [sic] Now the mother and daughter were all mine." Rees had underlined the last two words.

Rees was convicted of the murder of Harold and sentenced to life imprisonment, then convicted of the murders of Carroll and Janet Jackson and sentenced to death. The death penalty was commuted after the US Supreme Court declared capital punishment unconstitutional in 1972.

Although Rees was also suspected in the deaths of four women in the University of Maryland area, no evidence has linked him to those crimes. He died of natural causes in prison in 1995.

Q: What Kansas City flea market merchant collected not only primitive art but also sex slaves?

A: Robert Berdella was an openly gay man who was well liked in his neighborhood, but in the 1980s his house on the 4300 block of Charlotte Street in Kansas City, Missouri, was the site of rape, torture, murder, and dismemberment.

Berdella's MO was to pick up male sex workers or other young, vulnerable men and take them to his house, where he would drug, restrain, and sexually assault them. He tortured them in truly heinous ways that included beating them with pipes, injecting them with Drano and penicillin, dabbing bleach in their eyes, and applying electrodes. Then he would kill them, sometimes after a day but other times after several weeks, sometimes by a combination of bludgeoning and suffocation and other times simply by overdose.

Six men suffered this terrible fate before 22-year-old Christopher Bryson, wearing only a dog collar and with red welts around his wrists, ankles, and mouth, broke free and jumped from a second floor window.

The 39-year-old Berdella was arrested, and police officers quickly discovered the extent of the horrors that had occurred. They found a human head and part of a backbone belonging to Berdella's last victim, Larry Pearson, in the garden; the skull of victim Robert Sheldon; two envelopes of teeth; traces of blood in the basement; and a huge stack of Polaroids documenting Berdella's torturous acts.

In 1988, on the agreement that prosecutors wouldn't seek the death penalty, Berdella confessed to his crimes and received a life sentence without the possibility of parole. He died of a heart attack in prison in 2002.

Q: What serial killer had been a Mormon missionary?

A: Arthur Gary Bishop was a confessed pedophile who bludgeoned, shot, or strangled five young boys in Utah, but before all of that he served as a Mormon missionary in the Philippines. The Church of Latter Day Saints (LDS) excommunicated him, however, after a 1978 embezzlement conviction.

Bishop assumed the name Roger Downs and headed to Salt Lake City. His first murder victim was four-year-old Alonzo Daniels, lured to Bishop's apartment with the promise of candy. When Daniels cried for his mother, Bishop hit him on the head with a hammer and then drowned him. He later told police he had fondled the boy and mutilated his genitals before carrying the tiny body out of his apartment while his mother searched for him, screaming his name.

The next three victims were Kim Peterson (age 11), Danny Davis (4), and Troy Ward (6). His last and oldest victim was 13-year-old Graeme Cunningham, to whom he had offered $200 to pose naked.

Bishop was an acquaintance of the Cunningham family and lived near where the previous boys had been abducted, which led police to call him in for questioning. He quickly confessed to not only his alias but also the murders of all five of his victims. He showed authorities where he had buried the bodies—the first three in the desert at Cedar Fort and the last two at Big Cottonwood Creek.

Bishop blamed child pornography for giving him the desire to carry out violent fantasies on young boys. When he was arrested, he told police he would kill again.

"I get a sexual pleasure out of seeing them naked afterwards," Bishop said.

He was convicted on five counts of murder, among other charges, and sentenced to death. Bishop decided to forego all appeals and was ready to pay the ultimate price for his sins. The former Mormon named Bishop found religion again in prison and spent his last day reading LDS scripture.

Bishop was 36 years old when he was executed by lethal injection in 1988. His last words were, "Give my apologies to the families of the victims."

Q: Who was the Trailside Killer who stalked people near San Francisco state parks?

A: David Carpenter, the Trailside Killer, was also considered a suspect in the Zodiac Murders. He didn't begin killing until he was 49 years old, which is fairly late by serial killer time frames, but once he began in 1979 he killed at least six and possibly 10 people in the span of nine months.

Carpenter's violent streak had begun long before that, too. As a teenager, he was busted for child molestation, and then in 1960, at age 30, he took a woman into the woods, tied her up, beat her with a hammer, and stabbed her in the hand. He was convicted of assault with intent to commit murder and two counts of assault with a deadly weapon and was sentenced to 14 years in prison. He only served nine of those, but while he was there he was diagnosed with sociopathic personality disorder.

Upon his release he continued to attack women, raping and beating them, but he didn't murder until he killed Edda Kane on August 19, 1979. Carpenter's usual method was shooting—most often execution style, having the victims kneel and then shooting them in the head at point blank range—though he did stab one woman repeatedly. His killings continued uninterrupted by law enforcement through the end of March 1981, when he shot Stephen Haertle and Ellen Hansen. Haertle survived and was able to provide a description to police.

His next kill was Heather Scaggs on May 1, and because she had told her boyfriend she was going to buy a car from someone named David Carpenter, she saved the lives of countless others. When police met with Carpenter they noticed the resemblance to the composite sketch developed from Haertle's description, and Haertle was also able to pick Carpenter from a lineup.

Carpenter was arrested, and with a little detective work the gun he had used in three of the attacks was found.

At his first trial in 1984, Carpenter was convicted of two murders and sentenced to death; at his second trial on additional murders, he was found guilty of four more.

Carpenter is currently on death row at San Quentin State Prison in California.

Q: Who was the Vampire Killer of Sacramento?

A: Richard Trenton Chase was so named because he drank the blood of his victims. He also practiced cannibalism and necrophilia with the dead bodies.

Before his serial killing began, Chase spent time in a mental institution, having been involuntarily committed after he injected the blood of a rabbit into his veins and had to seek treatment for blood poisoning.

As a child, Chase would catch and kill animals to dissect them; he would also eat some of the animals raw or mix their organs with Coke in a blender as a refreshing beverage. Some of this pattern continued at the psychiatric hospital, where he frequently bit the heads off of birds to suck their blood. Chase was diagnosed with paranoid schizophrenia and was released with proper medication. Not long thereafter, unfortunately, his mother weaned him from the meds and sent him out on his own again.

Chase first killed 51-year-old Ambrose Griffin, in December 1977. Less than a month later he shot, raped, and stabbed 22-year-old Teresa Wallin, who was pregnant. He disemboweled her and drained her blood into a cup to drink it.

Chase's next victims were Evelyn Miroth (age 38), her son Jason (6), and friend Daniel Meredith (51). Miroth's 22-month-old nephew was missing but presumed dead because his playpen was bloody and a gun had been fired through a pillow.

Chase was apprehended based on the tip of a high school friend who saw him with blood on his clothes. Police found much evidence of cannibalism at his apartment, including blenders full of blood and organs in the refrigerator. The body of Miroth's nephew, decapitated, was found outside.

Chase pleaded not guilty by reason of insanity, but he was judged legally sane, found guilty, and sentenced to death. He would never meet his executioner, however. Chase stored his anti-depressant meds for weeks until he had a fatal dosage in his possession. He died by suicide on December 26, 1979.

Q: Who volunteered for psychiatric care three times before murdering at least 14 women?

A: Carroll Edward Cole, despite a genius IQ of 152, couldn't manage to keep himself off death row.

As a young boy, Cole was dragged along by his mother as she carried on adulterous trysts with men. Back at home, she beat him to make sure he kept his mouth shut. Moreover, he was relentlessly bullied at school for his "sissy" first name. All of this led to what he admitted was his first murder—the drowning of a bullying schoolmate when Cole was just eight years old.

As an adult, overcome by fantasies of raping and strangling women, he approached police officers to ask for psychiatric help. Cole spent a few years going in and out of mental institutions in the 1960s, but upon his release he moved from California to Texas and got married. The relationship was volatile, and the marriage ended in arson—he burned down a motel where he thought his wife was conducting liaisons. Cole was sent to prison.

After his release he attempted to murder an 11-year-old girl in Missouri and served several years in prison, but inmate psychiatric programs didn't much help him. Still experiencing mental health issues after his release, he voluntarily turned himself in again for psychiatric care, this time in Nevada—and doctors basically sent him off with a ticket to go to California.

Cole did go west, and he killed several women in California, another in Wyoming, one in Nevada, one in Oklahoma, and then at least one more in California before killing his second wife, Diana. Diana's body was found wrapped in a blanket in a closet, yet it was still ruled a "natural" death because she was an alcoholic.

Cole went back to Texas and killed at least three more women. Police were once again ready to let him go, but he started confessing to several unsolved murders.

Cole was undoubtedly ready to die. In 1981 he pleaded guilty in exchange for life imprisonment with the possibility of parole, but then he voluntarily faced murder charges in Nevada, knowing that the sentence would probably be death. And it was.

He discouraged anti-capital punishment protesters from fighting against his sentence and even thanked the judge for sending him to his death. A Roman Catholic, Cole made a final confession and took communion before being put to death by lethal injection at Nevada State Prison in 1985.

Q: What was serial killer Dean Corll's nickname, inspired by the family business?

A: Corll was known as the Candy Man—eerily appropriate, since he targeted children.

When he was a teenager, Corll worked in his mother's Houston candy factory, Pecan Prince. As an adult, he sometimes used candy to lure young boys into his white van, or a Plymouth GTX. At other times he trolled the streets of the Houston Heights neighborhood, offering his soon-to-be victims much harder candy in the forms of drugs and alcohol.

Back at his apartment, Corll would strip the boys and tie them to a homemade wooden rack, spread-eagled, to rape and torture them—sometimes for days—before shooting or strangling them.

One of the most disturbing aspects of Corll's story is that he hired two teenage accomplices to help him find victims. David Owens Brooks and Elmer Wayne Henley were paid $10 to $200 for each victim procured, and it wasn't until Corll turned on one of the boys that the murder ring was exposed.

Henley was just 17 years old when he called police on August 8, 1973, to tell them he had shot and killed 33-year-old Corll in self-defense during one of their lacquer-sniffing sex parties. Henley had brought another boy and a girl to the apartment, and the girl's presence angered Corll. He plied all three youth with marijuana and alcohol in addition to the intoxicating fumes, and once they had passed out he restrained them. Henley was able to convince Corll that he would help him torture the other two, but when he wanted to stop things he took Corll's .25 caliber revolver and turned it on him. The Candy Man dared him to shoot him, so he did—five times in all.

From there, Henley told authorities about the previous murders and showed them where the bodies had been left, escorting skeptical detectives to a boat storage unit and then to Lake Sam Rayburn and High Island Beach. A search of Corll's home revealed a plastic sheet covering the bedroom floor—hello, Dexter—and a toolbox containing various sex toys and devices.

In all, 27 boys died at the hands of the Candy Man and his cohorts between 1970 and 1973. The worst mass murder in recent US history at that time, the killings were known as the Houston Mass Murders. As of 2018, one victim remained unidentified.

Henley was convicted of six murders and sentenced to six consecutive 99-year prison terms. Brooks, who was 18 years old at the time of his arrest, was convicted of one murder and received a life sentence. The two have repeatedly come up for parole, only to be denied.

Q: What killer known as the Kansas City Strangler was caught by DNA from old crimes?

A: Lorenzo Gilyard might have gotten away with murder if it hadn't been for DNA preserved from former crimes. But his 1987 DNA was still talking in 2004 when crime lab workers tested evidence from unsolved murder cases and linked him with the deaths of 13 women. Gilyard argued that such evidence only proved he had had sex with the women—the majority of the victims were prostitutes—but the judge didn't go for that argument. He was found guilty on six of the seven murder charges leveled against him.

The state chose to bring only the seven strongest cases to trial, and six of them involved semen that matched Gilyard's. On the seventh charge, which Gilyard beat, the DNA link was through hairs found on victim Angela Mayhew's sweater.

The victims had all been found around Kansas City, Missouri, and were all killed in a similar manner, though details varied slightly, suggesting that the killer grabbed whatever was handy to carry out his murders. Evidence of ligature was present at many of the crime scenes, with some victims found with a shoestring or electrical cord wrapped around their necks. Others were strangled with bare hands. All of Gilyard's confirmed and suspected victims were found without shoes.

Gilyard wasn't a stranger to legal proceedings, having served time for the rape and beating of a 13-year-old girl. He also had convictions for aggravated assault for threatening to shoot his wife, and third-degree assault for viciously beating her after their divorce. Additionally, between 1969 and 1974 he was suspected in five rape cases, but no charges were ever filed.

In 2007 Gilyard agreed to a trial without a jury in exchange for the death penalty being removed as a possible punishment. And so, when he was convicted of the murders of six women, he was sentenced to life in prison without parole.

In 2018 Gilyard granted an interview with journalist Piers Morgan, continuing to profess his innocence and claim that the DNA evidence had been planted.

Q: Who served time for killing children, then was released and began murdering prostitutes?

A: Arthur Shawcross, the Genesee River Killer, said he was severely abused as a child by his mother and also had a sexual relationship with his sister. At age 21 he was drafted into the Vietnam War, and he claimed to have witnessed terrible atrocities, though his military record doesn't show that he saw any combat.

In any event, before committing his first murder in 1972, Shawcross was already an ex-con who had been released after serving nearly two years of a five-year arson sentence. Then he took 10-year-old Jack Owen Blake fishing in Watertown, New York. The boy's body was found in the woods months later; Shawcross had raped and killed him.

That same year, Shawcross raped and murdered eight-year-old Karen Ann Hill. This time witnesses had seen him with the little girl and were able to identify Shawcross.

He confessed to the two murders, but an inexplicably generous plea bargain shaved his charges down to manslaughter and a sentence of a mere 25 years. He was released on parole less than 15 years later, in 1987.

Shawcross moved to Rochester, and for the sake of anonymity, his criminal record was sealed so that his new community wouldn't freak out. There he began changing up his killing game. His new targets were prostitutes, and his method was strangulation. He dumped the women's bodies into the Genesee River.

Over the next year and a half, Shawcross killed 12 women; all but one were prostitutes. Although authorities were well aware that a serial killer was on the loose, routine checks of the criminal pasts of potential suspects didn't turn up Shawcross, since his record had been sealed. Then one day, detectives saw him on the Salmon Creek Bridge, near where his last victim had been found. They ran the plates on his nearby van and arrested him.

Shawcross submitted a lengthy confession and pleaded not guilty by reason of insanity. His defense failed, and he was convicted and sentenced to 250 years in prison. Shawcross died of natural causes in 2008.

Chapter 6

UNSOLVED/ ONGOING CASES

Q: Which of New York City's 40-some islands was stomping grounds for a serial killer?

A: Long Island. Nearly a dozen women have been murdered by the so-called Long Island Serial Killer (LISK) over a period of about 20 years, with dismembered bodies left off the Ocean Parkway, but he remains unidentified. Also called the Gilgo Killer because several victims were found near Gilgo Beach, he may have left the area—his last known victim died in 2010. Some, however, believe he was still killing as late as 2013.

LISK is sometimes also called the Craigslist Ripper because he found some of his victims through escort ads on that website. The stories of six victims are quite similar, in that the women disappeared after going to meet a stranger who promised cash in exchange for sexual services. Strangulation was the killing method of choice for LISK, and victims were sometimes dismembered.

Bodies began turning up in May 2010 after the disappearance of 24-year-old Shannan Gilbert in Oak Beach. Gilbert, who had been diagnosed as bipolar but wasn't taking medication, called 911 from the home of client Joseph Brewer, reportedly saying, "They're trying to kill me" (the recording has not been made public). Brewer's version is that Gilbert became frenetic without explanation so he asked her driver, Michael Pak, to help him calm her down. But the woman ran to the neighbors' house—and disappeared.

While searching for Gilbert, authorities found the remains of four other victims, including a mother and child; they were referred to as the Gilgo Four at the time. Five more bodies were later discovered.

Gilbert's body was eventually found as well, though some don't believe she was even a victim of LISK and that her death was a coincidence.

LISK's current profile says he is likely a white male in his 20s to 40s. He may have law enforcement knowledge or even work in the field—and may have access to burlap sacks as part of his employment, as several bodies were recovered in them.

Convicted serial killer Joel Rifkin, aka the Long Island Killer, has denied responsibility for the LISK crimes, and no evidence has linked him to the murders.

Some online sleuths point to ex-Suffolk County Police Chief James Burke as a possible suspect, but no evidence has tied him to the crimes. In 2016 Burke was sentenced to 46 months in a federal prison after beating a handcuffed man for stealing pornography and sex toys from Burke's car. That same year, an escort publicly claimed that Burke had paid her for sex in Oak Beach five years prior. Neither of these tidbits, though, provides substantiation for the claim that Burke and LISK are one and the same.

Carpenter John Bittrolff, convicted in 2017 of murdering two prostitutes in the 1990s, is another potential suspect. Bittrolff's victims were found about 35 miles from Gilgo Beach. He is serving two consecutive sentences of 25 years to life.

As of now, however, the identity of LISK remains a mystery.

Q: Who are the Rocky Mount Ten?

A: The Rocky Mount Ten are women believed to be the victims of a single murderer, the Edgecombe County Killer or Seven Bridges Killer, in the area of Rocky Mount, North Carolina. The victims were all poor, black sex workers with substance abuse problems. The killer disposed of their bodies along Seven Bridges Road.

Disappearances and murders had been happening for several years when finally, in 2009, authorities began connecting the dots between the murders and missing persons cases of women who shared common characteristics.

The first victim was 29-year-old Melody Wiggins, in 2005; her body was found near Nobles Mill Pond Road. Other victims include Jackie Nikelia ("Nikki") Thorpe (age 35), Taraha Sharice Nicholson (28), Jarniece "Sunshine" Hargrove (31), Ernestine Battle (50), Roberta Williams (40), Christine Boone (43), Elizabeth Jane Smallwood (33), and Yolanda Renee Lancaster (37). The remains of some of the victims weren't found until years after they had disappeared, making the investigation all the more challenging.

Forty-six-year-old Joyce Renee Durham, who went missing in 2007 and whose remains have not been found, is also a suspected victim of the Seven Bridges Killer.

Antwan Maurice Pittman, who is learning disabled and was charged with the attempted rape of a two-year-old when he was a teenager, was convicted of the murder of Nicholson in 2011, but the other eight cases of murder remain unsolved officially.

In 2009, on the night Sunshine Hargrove disappeared, a state trooper had happened upon a sleeping Pittman in his car along Seven Bridges Road—about 200 yards from where Hargrove's body was discovered years later. The trooper noted Pittman's unzipped pants and muddy boots, but Pittman got only a DUI charge and revocation of his driver's license.

Authorities say they are continuing to work on the open cases.

Q: What nickname was given to the killer of eight London prostitutes from 1959 and 1964?

A: Because of obvious similarities with one of the most famous serial killer cases of all time, the unidentified murderer is known as Jack the Stripper.

Known as the Hammersmith murders, the killings followed a general pattern: women were strangled or suffocated and left naked or almost so.

Several victims' four front teeth were pushed out or loose, leading one investigator to posit that they may have choked to death while performing oral sex. One victim was determined to have died while kneeling.

Among the only solid clues were paint chips found on some of the bodies and evidence that one woman had been stored in a warm place before being moved elsewhere.

Scotland Yard Chief Superintendent John Du Rose handled the case. Early in the investigation, detectives matched the paint chips with a sample found beneath a concealed transformer at the Heron Factory Estate in Aston; there was a spray-painting shop nearby. Du Rose identified 20 suspects, then 10, and finally three. One of those, Mungo Ireland, died by suicide, leaving a note that said "I can't stick it any longer."

The murders did stop—but the case officially remains unsolved, and amateur detectives have been pondering it ever since. Short of a confession, the chances of identifying Jack the Stripper are slim, as all the forensic evidence associated with the case is believed to have been lost or destroyed.

Q: What 1946 murders were named for the time of day they were committed?

A: The Moonlight Murders took place in Texarkana, Texas, where the so-called Phantom Killer or Phantom Slayer targeted lovers' lanes during the full moon. This was similar to what the Monster of Florence did in the Tuscan countryside two decades later, except that his Italian counterpart chose to kill on moonless nights.

The first targeted victims, Jimmy Hollis and Mary Larey, survived the February 1946 attack, in which Larey was raped and both were brutally beaten. The next month, however, Richard Griffin and Polly Ann Moore weren't so lucky; both were shot to death. And three weeks later, teens Paul Martin and Betty Jo Booker were shot after attending a dance.

At this point, Texas Rangers arrived on the scene. Residents of the city were on edge, many even hiding in their homes or simply leaving town until the killings stopped. And they did stop, at least on lovers' lanes. The last victim connected with the Phantom was Virgil Starks, gunned down while reading the evening newspaper in his farmhouse. Starks' wife fled for help while the gunman poked about the residence, leaving a trail of bloody footprints. He later dropped his two-cell flashlight outside, but otherwise the killer left no evidence behind.

Speculation that the murderer took his own life was rampant after a body was found on the railroad tracks a few days later. As it turned out, though, the dead man had been stabbed before being placed on the tracks. It is possible that poor Earl McSpadden was actually the Phantom's last victim, killed in a pathetic attempt to stage a suicide.

The identify of the Moonlight Murders perpetrator has never been confirmed, but the prime suspect has long been Youell Swinney. His own wife implicated him with incredibly comprehensive statements—including details new to the police—but wouldn't testify against him. Later she recanted. And so the Phantom remains elusive.

Q: Who is considered to be Hawaii's first serial killer?

A: The Honolulu Strangler murdered five women in 1985 and 1986—and remains unidentified, at least officially.

Sunny beaches in the land of rainbows are hardly the backdrop one imagines for a serial killer, but for two years Honolulu was just that.

The Honolulu Strangler chose women who weren't local and had few if any ties to the area. His victims—ages 17 to 36—had their hands bound behind their backs with rope before being raped and strangled. He left their bodies nude from the waist down.

He preferred to dispose of his victims' remains in isolated locations, and the extreme desolation of his final choice may, in a roundabout way, have led to his probable identification.

Linda Pesce had gone missing on April 29, 1986. Four days later a man contacted police to tell them that a psychic had told him that her body was on Honolulu's Sand Island. He led them to a specific spot, but she wasn't there. Eventually, however, Pesce's body was found on the island.

Unsurprisingly, the police narrowed in on this man as their primary suspect. Both his girlfriend and his ex-wife confirmed that he was into sexual bondage. The ex-wife noted that the murder dates coincided with fights they'd had—after which he would disappear all night. The suspect failed two polygraph tests, but without any further evidence linking him to the murders, authorities let him go. They still haven't been able to make an arrest in the case.

In May 2018, in an episode of the TV show *Breaking Homicide*, former prosecutor and Honolulu mayor Peter Carlisle put a name to the suspect: Howard Gay. Carlisle lamented the lack of DNA technology in the mid-80s, as he is convinced that with today's detection methods they would've gotten their man.

Gay has since passed away, and the identity of the Honolulu Strangler may never be established.

Q: What murders forever changed the way over-the-counter painkillers are sold?

A: The Tylenol Murders in Chicago took place over one terrifying week in 1982, beginning on September 29 with the death of 12-year-old Mary Kellerman of Elk Grove Village. She had taken an Extra-Strength Tylenol capsule and died quickly afterward. That same day, 27-year-old Adam Janus in Arlington Heights died unexpectedly, and then his 25-year-old brother and 19-year-old sister-in-law passed away as well. As it turned out, all had taken Extra-Strength Tylenol. Then three more people died in the greater Chicago area, and finally authorities identified the common denominator: Tylenol capsules laced with cyanide.

Johnson & Johnson immediately recalled the more than 30 million bottles of Extra-Strength Tylenol already out on shelves. Additional tainted bottles were found during the sweep, but no more deaths occurred.

Investigation revealed that the medication had been tampered with sometime after leaving the factory, which meant someone went to various stores around Chicago, lacing capsules with cyanide—or more likely, dropping already-laced capsules into the bottles.

Because of this deadly episode, Johnson & Johnson began producing smooth, easy-to-swallow caplets that looked like capsules but didn't break apart in the center, making them more difficult to tamper with. Also, manufacturers began placing foil seals over the tops of bottles.

No one was ever arrested in the deaths of the five Tylenol victims, and no solid suspects were ever identified. One man did attempt to claim responsibility and request a $1 million ransom from Johnson & Johnson, but law enforcement decided that James Lewis' letter was merely a hoax, as he was located in New York and had no ties to Chicago. Lewis did get an extortion conviction out of it, though, and served 13 years in prison for his trouble.

In 2009 the FBI looked more closely at Ted Kaczynski, the Unabomber, as a possible suspect, but the identity of the culprit remains unknown.

Q: What New Hampshire killer is thought responsible for the deaths of seven women?

A: The Connecticut River Valley Killer murdered at least seven women from the late 1970s to the late 1980s. But it wasn't until the mid-1980s, when the skeletal remains of three young women who had been missing for years were found around Claremont, New Hampshire, that authorities realized they probably had a serial killer on their hands. A closer look revealed that the women were likely stabbed to death, and they knew it was time to search the files for other area murders around that time.

The first murder linked with the man who became known as the Connecticut River Valley Killer was that of Cathy Millican, in October 1978. She had been stabbed repeatedly. In July 1981 a hitchhiking Mary Elizabeth Critchley vanished and wasn't found until weeks later, her body already in an advanced state of decomposition; no cause of death was decipherable.

At the end of May in 1984, 16-year-old Bernice Courtemanche disappeared while hitchhiking; her body turned up two years later. She had been stabbed in the neck and had a head injury. In July of the same year, Ellen Fried never made it home after a roadside phone chat with her sister, during which she noted a vehicle crawling slowly back and forth nearby. Her body was discovered months later with stab wounds; she was likely sexually assaulted as well.

In July 1985, Eva Morse disappeared while hitchhiking; her remains turned up a year later close to where Critchley's body had been found. In April 1986, the husband of Lynda Moore came home to find her bloody body. Moore had been stabbed, but this time witnesses were able to give enough information for police to draw up a composite sketch.

In January 1987, Barbara Agnew's car was found at a rest stop on I-91, just 10 miles from her home. Her body was located in Vermont months later, but why she stopped so close to home in a snowstorm remains a mystery.

The last attack attributed to the Connecticut River Valley Killer was the brutal stabbing of seven-month-pregnant Jane Boroski in August 1988. Boroski survived and was able to identify her assailant's vehicle—a Jeep Wagoneer—and provide details for a sketch.

A huge break may have come in 1997 when Gary Westover, a paraplegic on his deathbed, confessed his knowledge of Agnew's murder to his uncle, Howard Minnon. He named three friends he'd been with that night, but the names have not been released to the public. Could a paraplegic needing help in a snowstorm have caused Agnew to pull off the road so close to home?

Lynn-Marie Carty, a private investigator, believes she knows the name of at least one of those three friends: Michael Nicholaou. Carty was hired by the family of Nicholaou's first wife, Michelle, who vanished in 1988—a couple months after the last attack attributed to the Connecticut River Valley Killer. Nicholaou owned a Jeep Wagoneer back then. Carty showed Boroski his photo, and the serial killer's only survivor believes he was her attacker.

In 2005 Nicholaou, who had been traumatized by his service in Vietnam, shot and killed his second wife and stepdaughter and then turned the gun on himself.

Alas, the cases of the victims of the Connecticut River Valley Killer remain open.

Q: What name is given collectively to eight murdered Louisiana women?

A: The Jeff Davis 8 were killed between 2005 and 2009 in Louisiana's Jefferson (Jeff) Davis Parish. Their bodies had been dumped on roadsides or in the crawfish ponds and canals around Jennings, Louisiana. The cause of death varied from strangulation to stabbing to throat-slashing.

All of the victims, ages 17 to 30, came from South Jennings, considered the poor side of town, and they all knew one another. Jennings only has a population of 10,000, after all.

They had all had prior brushes with the law and worked in the sex trade, and the women had one overarching thing in common: they had been police informants regarding the local drug trade.

Allegations of improperly preserved crime scenes and an ineffective and even corrupt investigation swirl around the case—involving politicians and cops and a sex and drug den named the Boudreaux Inn. None of that inspires much hope that the murders will ever be solved.

Some people—such as investigative reporter Ethan Brown, author of *Murder in the Bayou: Who Killed the Women Known as the Jeff Davis 8?*—believe that there are several different killers and that this isn't a serial killer case at all.

The Jeff Davis 8 investigation is ongoing.

Q: What popular spring break locale was a serial killer's home base from 2005 to 2007?

A: Between December 2005 and February 2006, three sex workers were found murdered in Daytona Beach, Florida. Laquetta Gunther, Julie Green, and Iwana Patton had all been sexually assaulted and shot, and their bodies had been discarded with no attempt to hide them. DNA confirmed that a serial killer was at large.

That said, authorities didn't have much else to go on. Given their profession as sex workers, police believe the women willingly went with their killer either on foot or in a vehicle, but with no witnesses, the trail was ice cold. In fact, police thought the killer had probably left the area after the last murder in 2006.

But then came the death of Stacey Charlene Gage, whose body was found in early January 2008. Police believe she had been murdered at the beginning of the previous September. There were striking similarities between her case and those of the three Daytona Beach Killer victims, except that Gage had no criminal history of prostitution.

With that murder, the Daytona Beach Police Department renewed their efforts to find the killer. At traffic stops beginning in February 2008, they swabbed the mouths of men who matched the profile they had developed: white male, clean cut, employed, with a girl-friend or wife.

As of now, however, there have been no named suspects or arrests.

Q: Who was the child killer known for setting his victims on snow piles?

A: Michigan's Oakland County Child Killer (OCCK), also called the Babysitter, dressed his victims in clean, pressed clothes and positioned them on piles of snow as if they were sleeping.

The disconnect between the horrible acts the OCCK committed on the children and the way he left their lifeless bodies is astoundingly vile. The unidentified killer abducted and killed at least four children in the mid-1970s.

His first victim was 12-year-old Mark Stebbins, who disappeared on his way home from the American Legion on February 15, 1976. His body was found four days later; he had been sexually assaulted and strangled.

Jill Robinson, also 12, ran away from home after a disagreement with her mom just before Christmas that same year. She was shot in the face with a 12-gauge shotgun.

On January 2, 1977, 10-year-old Kristine Mihelich went missing after leaving a 7-Eleven convenience store. She was found 19 days later, smothered. Disturbingly, her autopsy showed that she had been murdered within the previous 24 hours, meaning that she had been kept captive that whole time.

A few months later, 11-year-old Timothy King disappeared. Witnesses later said they saw him get into a car they identified as a blue AMC Gremlin with a white racing stripe, with a man who had long, shaggy hair. King's body was discovered six days later, having been killed only within the previous six hours. He had been sexually assaulted and suffocated.

One of the main suspects was convicted pedophile Archibald Edward Sloan, currently serving a life sentence in Michigan. Hair samples taken from Sloan's car matched those found on the bodies of both Stebbins and King, but law enforcement didn't have enough evidence to hold him. Sloan claimed he often let his pedophile friends use his car. Years later, it was confirmed that Sloan had failed a polygraph test related to the murders.

Another prime suspect was Theodore Lamborgine, part of a multistate child pornography ring uncovered thanks to investigation into the OCCK murders. DNA exonerated him in the murders of King and Stebbins, however.

Then there was the son of a top executive at General Motors. Christopher Busch also dealt in child pornography and had been convicted of raping teen Vincent Gunnels, who was a childhood acquaintance of Busch's nephew. In 2011 a mitochondrial DNA match was found between Gunnels' hair and a hair found on victim Kristine Mihelich, but Gunnels insists he was only a victim of Busch and has no idea how it could have ended up there. In 1978 Busch died a suspicious death by gunfire, ruled a suicide despite there being no gunshot residue on his hands or any blood spatter in his apartment.

One intriguing tidbit is that the hair of the same white dog was found on all of the victims. Could that be the clue that finally traps the OCCK, with someone remembering who owned a white dog in the mid-1970s in or around Oakland County and was also (maybe) a murderous pedophile?

In February 2019, Investigation Discovery aired a two-part series called *Children of the Snow* in the hopes that someone, somewhere will speak up about something they now remember, and hopefully get these cold cases solved.

Q: Why was a series of child killings in the early 1970s called the Alphabet Murders?

A: The three young victims killed in the Rochester, New York area were Carmen Colon (age 10), Michelle Maenza (11), and Wanda Walkowicz (11). Because each victim had matching first and last initials, the killings were dubbed the Alphabet Murders or the Double Initial Murders. Although there have been several suspects in the killings, there has never been an arrest.

Even more weird, each girl was found in a town that began with the same letter as her initials—Colon in Churchville, Maenza in Macedon, and Walkowicz in Webster.

One suspect was Hillside Strangler Kenneth Bianchi, who was an ice cream vendor in Rochester at the time the girls were raped and murdered. He has never been formally excluded as a suspect; in fact, witnesses may have placed his car at two of the murder scenes.

This unsolved case has a strange connection with a series of murders in Los Angeles that were also called Alphabet or Double Initial Murders for the same reason. In fact, young Carmen Colon shared her name with an adult Carmen Colon who was a victim in the LA murders, for which serial killer Joseph Naso was convicted and sentenced to death. Naso was a native of Rochester, but DNA evidence excluded him from consideration in the New York murders.

A 1995 *Los Angeles Times* article teased that authorities may have gotten a lead from an inmate who knew the identity of the killer and that he was "still living in this region on Lake Ontario's southern shore." But no information seems to have emerged publicly from that proclamation, despite the promise that evidence was being turned over to the FBI crime laboratory.

And so the identity of the Alphabet Killer of Rochester remains unknown.

Q: What nickname was given to the killer who buried victims in the New Mexico desert?

A: The West Mesa Bone Collector disposed of his victims' remains on West Mesa within Albuquerque, New Mexico. In February 2009, a woman walking her dog near 118th Street made the gruesome discovery of a human bone protruding from the desert. It took weeks, but police eventually uncovered the remains of 11 women and one fetus strewn across the isolated 92-acre stretch of land. Identifying the victims took almost another year.

Authorities believe that all the victims were murdered between 2001 and 2005. The girls and young women ranged in age from 15 to 32. Most were Hispanic and worked as prostitutes, and many had also been involved with drugs. Unfortunately, these qualities surely led to less media coverage than the case should have gotten. Leads have been sparse in Albuquerque's worst-ever incidence of mass murder, dubbed "the crime of the century" in local media.

The lack of publicity only compounded the fact that advanced decomposition meant that medical examiners couldn't determine the causes of death, and virtually no DNA evidence was even recoverable.

The strongest suspect in the case was Lorenzo Montoya, but he's not around to talk anymore. Montoya met his demise in 2006 when he hired a prostitute to come to his home, tied her up, and strangled her. Apparently Montoya wasn't aware that her boyfriend had been waiting outside. When she didn't come out at the scheduled time, the boyfriend went in and ended up killing Montoya in self-defense. Montoya lived near the West Mesa and had been arrested for attempting to strangle a prostitute in 1999. After Montoya's death there were no more murders associated with the Bone Collector.

Other suspects include convicted murderer Scott Lee Kimball (now deceased), a pimp who reportedly searched for Bone Collector victims before anyone knew they were missing, and convicted child rapist Joseph Blea, whose wife and ex-wife have said they believe he's the killer. Then there are the anonymous calls to private investigator George Walker, taunting him with promised but never delivered information.

Technically, the homicide investigation continues, but without someone coming forward with more information, it's difficult to imagine how much progress is possible.

Q: What was the Freeway Phantom's preferred dumping ground?

A: The killer favored leaving his victims' bodies alongside I-295 in Washington, DC. The deaths of six girls ranging in age from 10 to 18 were attributed to the Freeway Phantom in the early 1970s; all had been raped and strangled.

The only real clue was a handwritten note shoved into the pocket of the fifth victim, 18-year-old Brenda Woodard. The note expressed the killer's "insensitivity [sic] to people especially women," and taunted police, "I will admit the others when you catch me if you can!" It was signed "Free-way Phantom."

The only serious suspects considered were members of the Green Vega Rapists, a gang responsible for a series of rapes in the area. A crumb of a lead emerged when one incarcerated member offered information about the killer, but only if his identity was kept secret. The promise was made, and the information was deemed credible because it included details that had not been made public. That particular inmate had a solid alibi, so he was cleared as a suspect. When he felt the secret of his identity was in jeopardy, though, he clammed up and denied having said anything in the first place.

Authorities still don't appear to have a firm suspect, and many of the case files have been lost—which makes it unlikely that this one will ever be solved.

Q: Who tried to pin down Cleveland's Mad Butcher of Kingsbury Run after pursuing Al Capone in Chicago?

A: Eliot Ness is best known for his work with the Prohibition Bureau for Chicago during the early 1930s, during which time he pursued the Mafia's highest order, including legendary gangster Al Capone. Just after that stint, Ness was hired as the Public Safety Director of Cleveland—and he immediately faced the mystery of unexplained dismembered bodies showing up along the Kingsbury Run section of the city.

The Mad Butcher of Kingsbury Run began his string of 12 to 20 murders in 1935 and continued through 1938. The killer targeted both men and women, with the common denominator being the fact that victims were usually transients, thus less likely to be missed. In fact, 10 of the confirmed 12 victims are still unidentified today.

The killings are alternately called the Cleveland Torso Murders because the perpetrator sometimes cut the victim cleanly in half. Each victim was beheaded, and many of the heads were never found. Most male victims were emasculated, and some of the bodies showed evidence of a chemical substance on the skin. Unfortunately, many of the bodies were already in an advanced state of decomposition when found, making identification nearly impossible—particularly in that time period.

The killer enjoyed taunting police, especially Ness, who had become the most famous lawman in the country thanks to his work on the Capone case. On one occasion the Mad Butcher situated the remains of two victims within view of Ness' office.

On August 18, 1938, Ness gave the go-ahead to raid the shantytown area of Kingsbury Run. He tramped through along with 35 police officers, rounding up more than 60 men. The next morning Ness ordered the empty shacks burned to the ground. That decision was widely criticized, but the Cleveland Torso Murders did stop.

Two suspects emerged, and one was even arrested. Frank Dolezal was brought in as the possible killer of victim Florence Polio, but he died in jail under mysterious circumstances six weeks after his arrest. The other potential perp was Dr. Francis Sweeney, who had performed amputations during World War I. He reportedly failed two polygraph exams, and Ness himself interviewed him. But Sweeney voluntarily committed himself to a mental institution, and nothing further ever came of that lead.

In December 1938, a few months after the last body was found, the chief of police received a typed noted from someone claiming to be the killer, saying that he had moved to California for the winter and had obtained a "volunteer" for his further studies. The writer said that he had been performing medical experiments on victims, referring to them as "laboratory guinea pigs found on any street." He added that although he was called a butcher, "the truth will out."

Yeah, it hasn't, and the Mad Butcher's identity remains a mystery.

Q: What gruesome nickname was given to the killer of young boys in New York City?

A: Charlie Chop-off—ugh—severed the penises of his victims. This officially unidentified murderer killed four children, three black and one Puerto Rican, and injured another between March 1972 and August 1973.

The first was eight-year-old Douglas Owens, who had been stabbed repeatedly; his penis had been cut but not severed. Next were nine-year-olds Wendel Hubbard and Louis Ortiz, killed five months apart. Both were stabbed repeatedly and had their penises severed. Seven-year-old Steven Cropper, the last known victim, was cut so badly with a razor blade that he bled to death. Though the depraved killer didn't emasculate him, he did carve a large "X" into the boy's chest.

Although these cases are technically unsolved, police have a solid suspect in Erno Soto, who was arrested after he tried and failed to abduct a Puerto Rican boy in May 1974. An addict who had been in and out of mental institutions, Soto confessed to the murder of Cropper and was brought to trial in 1976 but found not guilty by reason of insanity. A psychiatrist testified that Soto was a "walking time bomb."

According to court documents, Soto had been on a weekend pass from a mental hospital when he murdered Cropper. In 1972 and 1973 during the times of the other murders, Soto was an outpatient at the Dunlap-Manhattan Psychiatric Center.

Further bolstering the idea that Soto is the culprit in all of these murders, one survivor said that Soto resembled his assailant. The police described the perpetrator as Hispanic, between 5'6" and 5'10", slim with dark hair and acne scars, and walking "with a strange gait, almost like a limp."

Still, the cases remain officially unsolved, and Soto's mental state means that legal closure is unlikely.

Q: How was the Grim Sleeper serial killer caught?

A: Lonnie David Franklin, Jr., was linked to the Grim Sleeper murders through a familial DNA search in a California offender database—the first successful use of such identification.

When DNA from Grim Sleeper crime scenes was entered into the system, it matched up with a sample from Franklin's son Christopher, on file because of a 2009 felony weapons possession charge. Authorities were then able to link Franklin directly through his own DNA, obtained by testing a discarded pizza crust, plate, and cup that police had nabbed after Franklin left a Los Angeles restaurant.

The Grim Sleeper got his nickname because of the lengthy lapse between murders—from 1988 to 2002. Serial killers rarely take that much time off between killings, so questions remain as to whether Franklin lay dormant all that time or just hasn't been officially linked with any of the unsolved murders that plagued Los Angeles during the 14-year hiatus. It is thought that the Grim Sleeper may ultimately be responsible for 100 deaths that are still under investigation.

The killer targeted black prostitutes. Franklin's first confirmed victim was Debra Jackson, in 1985. He shot her three times in the chest and then used the same gun in nine more murders, though sometimes he strangled his victims instead. Enietra Washington survived getting shot and raped in 1988, and she was able to identify Franklin once police had identified him.

In Franklin's home, police found upwards of 1,000 photographs of women and young girls in various states of life and death, some nude, some bloodied.

In 2016 Franklin was convicted on nine counts of murder and sentenced to death. That may feel like closure to his case, but when you consider that the man his neighbors described as friendly and generous may have killed 11 times that many women, things don't feel quite so settled. That's why the case of the Grim Sleeper, also called the Southside Slayer, is ongoing.

Q: Who was imprisoned for one of the Atlanta Ripper murders but probably wasn't guilty?

A: Charlie Owens was convicted of the crime, but the murders didn't end with his imprisonment. In fact, they got even more brutal.

The Atlanta Ripper, like his better-known counterpart Jack the Ripper in London, attacked women, but his murders never received the same volume of press. Not even close. Between 1911 and 1915, the Atlanta Ripper targeted African Americans at a time when white-owned newspapers weren't particularly interested even in the brutal mass murder of black and mixed-race women.

Indeed, it wasn't until the Ripper claimed his eighth victim that news of the murders made the front page of the *Atlanta Constitution*. Sadie Holley's battered body was found with her head smashed in by a rock, found later, bloody, where it had been tossed aside. Her throat had been slashed from one ear to the other, as was the Ripper's signature by that point.

The newspaper acknowledged that the murders had been going on for some time by listing all of the previous victims. It was also noted that Atlanta's black pastors were calling on the mayor and the governor of Georgia to offer a reward for the killer's capture.

One of the most frightening encounters with the Ripper was that of Emma Lou Sharpe, who ran into a tall black man in a wide-brimmed black hat just after he had killed her mother, Lena. The stranger told her not to worry—"I never hurt girls like you"—and then plunged a knife into her back. Emma Lou survived, and the man disappeared into the shadows as her neighbors ran to help her.

In addition to Owens, four other men were arrested under suspicion of being the Ripper. Todd Henderson and Henry Huff were found not guilty, and a man named John Daniel appears to have been indicted but never brought to trial. Each time, with the accused man in custody, the murders continued. At one point authorities were convinced that the Ripper was a white man disguised as a black man, though newspaper accounts from the time make it hard to believe they had any sort of grip on what was happening.

It appears law enforcement simply lucked out when the murders stopped in 1915, as they didn't seem any closer to solving the case than they were when the murders had begun four years earlier. In all, the Atlanta Ripper may have claimed as many as 21 lives. More than a hundred years later, it's unlikely that the victims will ever receive justice.

Q: Who were the main targets of the Axeman of New Orleans?

A: Italian grocers seemed to be singled out for the Axeman's wrath from May 1918 to October 1919. As the moniker suggests, the Axeman used an axe to kill his victims. He broke into several Italian groceries using a railroad shoe pin and simply grabbed the available axe from the wall—back then it was a common tool to have handy—and slaughtered one or more occupants. Sometimes he also used a razor.

Nothing was ever stolen, so the goal wasn't robbery. To this day no one really knows what drove the Axeman to murder, but at least a dozen deaths have been attributed to him.

One theory is that the killings were racially motivated. As one of the newer immigrant groups to arrive in the country, southern Italians in the early 20th century faced much discrimination, just as waves of immigrants before them had. Many northern Italians had arrived decades before and were more assimilated, but the darker skin of southern Italians brought about the basest of antagonistic feelings in some Americans.

At the beginning of the 20th century, New Orleans had one of the largest Sicilian communities in America. They were considered by some to be "black dagoes," a derogatory term all around, and even faced lynch mobs. At the same time, Sicilians prospered economically by running businesses such as groceries within their own community. Accordingly, some believe the Axeman had a figurative axe to grind with Sicilians.

One of the oddest factoids in this case is that the Axeman loved jazz music and promised not to kill anyone playing it in their homes on March 19, 1919—St. Joseph's Day, an important holiday in Italian communities. It was also Father's Day in Italy. Jazz blared through the streets that night, and no one was killed.

The Axeman seems to have left New Orleans in late 1919, only to move on to other parts of Louisiana—where more Italian grocers were attacked in 1920 and 1921. And that's where the Axeman's story ends, as no suspects were ever brought to justice.

Q: What Virginia road was the backdrop for murder from 1986 to 1989?

A: Virginia's Colonial Parkway Murders of four couples have been well publicized in the media, but the perpetrator is still unknown.

The killer targeted one couple at a time, starting in October 1986 with US Naval Academy graduate Cathleen Thomas and College of William & Mary senior Rebecca Ann Dowski. The women were bound and strangled and had their throats slashed. Their vehicle had been doused in diesel, though it failed to light. No money or valuables were taken, and there were no signs of sexual assault. Thomas did manage to get a clump of the attacker's hair in her hand in the struggle; perhaps someday that can lead to DNA identification.

Almost an entire year later, David Knobling and Robin Edwards were found along the James River near Smithfield, Virginia. They had been shot to death. Six months after that, in April 1988, college students Cassandra Lee Hailey and Richard Keith Call went missing, and their bodies have never been located. They are presumed to have fallen victim to the Colonial Parkway killer, as their car was found abandoned at an overlook along the road.

In October 1989, the bodies of Annamaria Phelps and Daniel Lauer, already in a state of advanced decomposition, were found by hunters in the woods not far from a rest area on Interstate 64. The couple had gone missing during Labor Day weekend a month and a half earlier.

Investigators really haven't had much to go on in the case—especially with no eyewitnesses of even any vehicle that might be involved. In

July 2018 a ray of hope appeared via a Facebook page entry by Bill Thomas, brother of victim Cathleen:

> #FBI and #VirginiaStatePolice have told the Colonial Parkway Murders families that we have potential perpetrator #DNA in 3 of the 4 #ColonialParkwayMurders crime scenes. There is no word on whether any of the samples overlap, and no matches so far as testing continues.

In March 2019, however, Thomas tweeted that the families hadn't received any further update in the previous 16 months.

So here we are. Sigh.

Q: What types of victims were targeted by the I-70 Killer in 1992?

A: Store clerks were the targets of killings in a month-long spree across the Midwest. The first murder was on April 8, when the killer shot a Payless Shoe Source manager in Indianapolis. Robin Fuldauer was alone in the store and was killed in broad daylight.

Just a few days later the killer made his way to a bridal shop in Wichita, Kansas and killed Patricia Magers, the store owner, and Patricia Smith. The shop was open past its usual time because a pickup was scheduled; the women opened the door for the killer, thinking he was their customer. Instead, they were already dead when the actual client arrived. For some reason the killer let the man go, and he gave police information for a composite sketch.

The next victim was in Terre Haute, Indiana, and authorities believe that killing may have been a mistake. The name on the shop was Sylvia's Ceramics, so it's likely the killer believed a woman would be working inside. Moreover, Michael McCown had his back to the door and wore his hair in a ponytail, so it's possible the killer assumed he was a woman when he shot him.

On May 4 the I-70 Killer was in St. Charles, Missouri, where he killed Nancy Kitzmiller in a boot store. Three days later he shot reflexologist Sarah Blessing in Raytown's Store of Many Colors, ending the spree— except that authorities believe the same murderer may be responsible for two killings and an attempted murder in Texas in 1993 and 1994.

The one link between all the murders is that the I-70 Killer used a semiautomatic .22 caliber weapon—and polished his bullets with jeweler's rouge, making for a smoother slide into the chamber. Ergo: he was probably someone who knew his way around a gun, for whatever that's worth. There was no sexual element to the crimes, and with the small amount of cash available at the stores he targeted, robbery doesn't seem like a primary motive (though he did steal some cash).

The police describe their suspect as a thin white man in his twenties or thirties, 5'7" to 5'8", with sandy blond or reddish hair and "lazy eyelids." Of course, this describes him as he looked in the mid-1990s. There's no telling what he looks like today—if he's still alive.

REFERENCES

Aamodt, M. G. "Serial Killer Statistics." September 4, 2016. http://maamodt
.asp.radford.edu/serial killer information center/project description.htm.

Berkshire Eagle. "Serial Child Killer Sentenced Again." June 18, 2008.
https://www.newspapers.com/image/533943919.

Berry-Dee, Christopher. *Female Serial Killers: Up Close and Personal.*
Berkeley: Ulysses Press, 2010.

Berry-Dee, Christopher. *Serial Killers: Up Close and Personal.* Berkeley:
Ulysses Press, 2002.

Bugliosi, Vincent and Curt Gentry. "Arrested in Raid on Ranch; Susan
Atkins Can't Keep Quiet." The Des Moines Register. January 27, 1975.
https://www.newspapers.com/image/338900891.

Carl Panzram Papers, 1928-1980. Retrieved May 19, 2019 from
https://scua2.sdsu.edu/archon/?p=collections/controlcard&id=366.

Cawthorne, Nigel. *Serial Killers & Mass Murderers.* Berkeley: Ulysses Press,
2007.

Cooksey, Katie. "Austrians Outraged Over 'Death Angels' Release." *The
Guardian*. July 18, 2008. https://www.theguardian.com/world/2008/
jul/18/austria.

CrimeMuseum.org. "Volkswagen Owned by Ted Bundy." Accessed May
19, 2019. https://www.crimemuseum.org/crime-library/artifacts/
volkswagen-owned-by-ted-bundy.

Crockett, Zachary. "What Data on 3,000 Murderers and 10,000 Victims
Tell Us about Serial Killers." December 2, 2016. https://www.vox.com/
2016/12/2/13803158/serial-killers-victims-data.

Douglas, John E. and Mark Olshaker. *Mindhunter: Inside the FBI's Elite Serial
Crime Unit.* New York: Gallery Books, 2017.

Eyman, Scott. "Ed Gein: Hollywood's Favorite Killer." *The Palm Beach Post.* February 16, 1991. https://www.newspapers.com/image/130204063.

Gettleman, Jeffrey. "As Victims' Relatives Watch, Nurse Who Killed 29 Gets 11 Life Terms." *New York Times.* March 3, 2006. https://www.nytimes.com/2006/03/03/nyregion/as-victims-relatives-watch-nurse-who-killed-29-gets-11-life-terms.html.

Haines, Max. "They Died at the Hands of Their Butler." *Nanaimo Daily News.* September 21, 1980. https://www.newspapers.com/image/324900831.

Hickey, Eric W. *Serial Murderers and Their Victims.* Boston: Cengage Learning, 2015.

Hoge, Steven K. "Competence to Stand Trial." *Indian Journal of Psychiatry* 58, Suppl. 2 (2016): S187–S190. https://www.ncbi.nlm.nih.gov/pmc/articles/PMC5282614.

Innes, Brian. *Serial Killers: Shocking, Gripping True Crime Stories of the Most Evil Murderers.* London: Quercus Editions Ltd, 2006 (updates by Nigel Cawthorne in 2017).

Johnston, Joni E. "Five Myths About Female Serial Killers." March 8, 2018. https://www.psychologytoday.com/us/blog/the-human-equation/201803/five-myths-about-female-serial-killers.

Lightning Guides, *Serial Killers: Jack the Ripper to the Zodiac Killer.* Berkeley: Lightning Guides, 2015.

Los Angeles Times. "'Dreamboat' Killed in Escape Attempt." December 18, 1974. https://www.newspapers.com/image/386181104.

McNamara, Michelle. *I'll Be Gone in the Dark: One Woman's Obsessive Search for the Golden State Killer.* New York: HarperCollins Publishers, 2018.

Malnic, Eric. "Slayer of LA Prostitutes Kills Himself in Austrian Prison Cell." *Los Angeles Times.* June 30, 1994. https://www.newspapers.com/image/158662160.

March, William. *The Bad Seed.* New York: Rinehart & Company, 1954.

Martin, John Bartlow. "The Master of Murder Castle." *Harper's.* December 1943. https://harpers.org/archive/1943/12/the-master-of-the-murder-castle.

Mitri, Lysée. "Suspected Killer David Parker Ray's Girlfriend Readies for Release." KRQE. September 28, 2017. https://www.krqe.com/news/

investigations/suspected-killer-david-parker-rays-girlfriend-readies-for-release_20180104025202434/900254338.

Morton, Robert J. "Serial Murder: Multi-Disciplinary Perspectives for Investigators." Accessed May 19, 2019. https://www.fbi.gov/stats-services/publications/serial-murder.

NBC News. "Police: 1981 Killing of Adam Walsh Solved." December 16, 2008. http://www.nbcnews.com/id/28257294/ns/us_news-crime_and_courts/t/police-killing-adam-walsh-solved/#.XOXSCtNKhE4.

Newton, Michael. *The Encyclopedia of Serial Killers*. New York: Checkmark Books, 2006.

O'Malley, Jaclyn. "Arrest Reveals Challenges of Serial Killing Cases." *Reno Gazette-Journal*. April 17, 2011. https://www.newspapers.com/image/148321222.

"A Real 'Mrs. Bluebeard.'" *The San Francisco Examiner*. August 9, 1925. https://www.newspapers.com/image/457615875.

Rosewood, Jack and Rebecca Lo. *The Big Book of Serial Killers*. LAK Publishing, 2017.

Ryan, Kori. "The Macdonald Triad: Predictor of Violence or Urban Myth?" (M.S. thesis, California State University, Fresno, 2009). https://digitized.library.fresnostate.edu/digital/collection/thes/id/37222.

San Francisco Examiner. "Former Police Chief Pens Memoirs on 'Zebra Murders.'" November 13, 2006. https://www.newspapers.com/image/462409398.

Schecter, Harold and Everitt, David. *The A to Z Encyclopedia of Serial Killers*. New York: Pocket Books, 2006.

Spiegel, Irving. "Link Hinted in Harlem and East Side Slayings." *New York Times*. August 20, 1973. https://www.nytimes.com/1973/08/20/archives/link-hinted-in-harlem-and-east-side-slayings-neighbors-of-boy.html.

Stanton, Sam. "Sacramento Cops Arrested Golden State Killer Suspect in 1996, Then Let Him Go." *Sacramento Bee*. March 15, 2019. https://www.sacbee.com/news/state/california/article227901874.html.

Times and Democrat. "Gaskins Given 2nd Life Term." April 28, 1977. https://www.newspapers.com/image/130204063.

Vronsky, Peter. *Serial Killers: The Method and Madness of Monsters*. New York: Berkeley Publishing, 2004.

Wang, Linda. "From 'Unabomber' to 'Mad Bomber,' a Look at Past Serial Bombers." March 21, 2018. https://www.npr.org/2018/03/21/595225573/from-unabomber-to-mad-bomber-a-look-at-past-serial-bombers.

Watts, Sarah. "Why Are There More Serial Killers in the US Than in Any Other Country?" May 14, 2018. https://www.aetv.com/real-crime/why-more-serial-killers-in-us-than-other-countries.

West, Don. "Is Santa Cruz the Capital of Murder?" *San Francisco Examiner*. February 18, 1973. https://www.newspapers.com/image/460601726.

Worthington, Roger. "Dahmer May Have Stopped Killing If He Had Zombie, Doctor Says." *Chicago Tribune*. February 11, 1992. https://www.chicagotribune.com/news/ct-xpm-1992-02-11-9201130508-story.html.

ACKNOWLEDGMENTS

Writing a book about serial killers had never occurred to me until I received a fateful email from editor extraordinaire, Casie Vogel. Thank you Casie, for bringing me this opportunity and for making the process of delivering my first book baby to the world as painless as possible— even fun! Huge thanks to everyone at Ulysses Press, in fact.

I am also forever grateful to my many sources of emotional support from all over the world-- so many friends and family who were always there with a message or meme or article about serial killers to keep me motivated. Thank you Mark Zuckerberg, for inventing Facebook and putting so many amazing people at my fingertips.

Bottom-of-my-heart thank yous:

To my mom, who couldn't be as present as she would have liked during this process but whose strength and persistence have always been my driving inspiration;

To Laura, my Amalfi Coast cheerleader who never put down her pom-poms even as she trudged through her own book-writing experience;

And to my daughter Marisa, who is still trying to figure out why anyone would want to kill cereal.

ABOUT THE AUTHOR

A native of Pennsylvania's Anthracite Coal Region, **Michelle Kaminsky** is a freelance writer with a law degree. She has been fascinated with true crime ever since watching the terrible re-creations of "Unsolved Mysteries." She is a graduate of Duke University and Temple University James E. Beasley School of Law and a senior contributor at *Forbes*. Her hobbies include listening to true crime podcasts, reading true crime books, and playing My Little Pony with her daughter (a lot). You can find her @michkaminsky just about everywhere on social media.